Chevy DIFFERENTIALS

HOW TO REBUILD
THE 10- and 12-BOLT

Jefferson Bryant

CarTech®

CarTech®

CarTech®, Inc.
39966 Grand Avenue
North Branch, MN 55056
Phone: 651-277-1200 or 800-551-4754
Fax: 651-277-1203
www.cartechbooks.com

Layout by Monica Seiberlich

ISBN 978-1-61325-161-4
Item No. SA310

Library of Congress Cataloging-in-Publication Data Available

Written, edited, and designed in the U.S.A.
Printed in China
10 9 8 7 6 5 4 3 2 1

Front Cover: General Motors equipped select muscle cars and certain trucks with the Chevy 12-bolt axle assembly. This proven limited-slip axle delivers exceptional durability and traction. It is also relatively easy and straightforward to rebuild. (Photo Courtesy Tony E. Huntimer)

Title Page: You can see the Chevy 10-bolt carrier inside the axle housing. When disassembling a limited-slip differential, you remove the C-Clip to remove the axle shafts.

Back Cover Photos

Top Left: The center pin is a potential failure point for the carrier. In this case, the pin broke around the locking bolt hole, allowing it to slide out. Luckily, the driver was just barely rolling and the differential was not under an enormous load, otherwise much more damage could have been done. When the pin came out, it locked up the differential. This could have split the case of the housing if it had happened at speed.

Top Right: Ring gears convert the engine's rotation to forward motion, but there is more to selecting a gear set than just what size you think you need.

Bottom Left: The spring pack is used to keep the tension on the clutches. Most GM limited-slips use four springs and two plates, but some use an S-spring. You can tune the level of slippage with the springs. Stock Eaton GM limited-slip differentials use 400-pound springs.

Bottom Right: Here is a bad wear pattern, showing that the pinion is too close to the ring gear. Note the hard edge on the coast side; it looks like a shark fin. This would be very noisy and generate a lot of heat. The answer is a thinner pinion shim.

OVERSEAS DISTRIBUTION BY:

PGUK
63 Hatton Garden
London EC1N 8LE, England
Phone: 020 7061 1980 • Fax: 020 7242 3725
www.pguk.co.uk

Renniks Publications Ltd.
3/37-39 Green Street
Banksmeadow, NSW 2109, Australia
Phone: 2 9695 7055 • Fax: 2 9695 7355
www.renniks.com

CONTENTS

ACKNOWLEDGMENTS

A special thanks goes out to all those who were helpful with this project: Randy's Ring and Pinion, Strange Engineering, Moser Engineering, Yukon Gear & Axle, Eaton, Mickey Thompson, Global West, RaTech, Summit Racing, Classic Performance Parts, Stainless Steel Brakes Corporation, Royal Purple, Chris Alston's Chassisworks, Vintage Wheel Works, Pat Mcelreath, Clayton Howard, Chris Franklin, and Charlie Fox.

INTRODUCTION

GM performance differentials are typically divided into the two types: the 10-bolt and the 12-bolt. The reality, however, is much more detailed than that. There are numerous "10-bolt" rear ends, and two "12-bolt" units; each has its own benefits and drawbacks. The purpose of this book is to help you determine which type of housing you have, what you need for your application, and most important, how to rebuild it.

In this book, I cover identification, inspection, parts selection, disassembly, modification, assembly, and proper setup. The key to any rear differential build is in the setup. Gear mesh and pinion depth are crucial to ensure a long life for your new parts.

If you select the wrong parts and gear ratios for your application, you could make things worse. Here, you will find details on how to select the proper gears for your application, including how tires affect the gearing and how power is transferred to forward motion. A chapter is included on drivelines, along with features on brakes so that you have the most accurate information needed to make the right decisions on parts.

WHAT IS A WORKBENCH® BOOK?

This Workbench® Series book is the only book of its kind on the market. No other book offers the same combination of detailed hands-on information and close-up photographs to illustrate rebuilding and modifying. Rest assured, you have purchased an indispensable companion that will expertly guide you, one step at a time, through each important stage of the rebuilding process. This book is packed with real-world techniques and practical tips for expertly performing rebuild procedures, not vague instructions or unnecessary processes. At-home mechanics or enthusiast builders strive for professional results, and the instruction in our Workbench® Series books help you realize pro-caliber results. Hundreds of photos guide you through the entire process from start to finish, with informative captions containing comprehensive instructions for every step of the process.

The step-by-step photo procedures also contain many additional photos that show how to install high-performance components, modify stock components for special applications, or even call attention to assembly steps that are critical to proper operation or safety. These are labeled with unique icons. These symbols represent an idea, and photos marked with the icons contain important, specialized information.

Here are some of the icons found in Workbench® books:

Important!
Calls special attention to a step or procedure, so that the procedure is correctly performed. This prevents damage to a vehicle, system, or component.

Save Money
Illustrates a method or alternate method of performing a rebuild step that will save money but still give acceptable results.

Torque Fasteners
Illustrates a fastener that must be properly tightened with a torque wrench at this point in the rebuild. The torque specs are usually provided in the step.

Special Tool
Illustrates the use of a special tool that may be required or can make the job easier (caption with photo explains further).

Performance Tip
Indicates a procedure or modification that can improve performance. The step most often applies to high-performance or racing engines.

Critical Inspection
Indicates that a component must be inspected to ensure proper operation of the engine.

Precision Measurement
Illustrates a precision measurement or adjustment that is required at this point in the rebuild.

Professional Mechanic Tip
Illustrates a step in the rebuild that non-professionals may not know. It may illustrate a shortcut or a trick to improve reliability, prevent component damage, etc.

Documentation Required
Illustrates a point in the rebuild where the reader should write down a particular measurement, size, part number, etc. for later reference or photograph a part, area, or system of the vehicle for future reference.

Tech Tip
Tech Tips provide brief coverage of important subject matter that doesn't naturally fall into the text or step-by-step procedures of a chapter. Tech Tips contain valuable hints, important info, or outstanding products that professionals have discovered after years of work. These will add to your understanding of the process, and help you get the most power, economy, and reliability from your engine.

HISTORY AND IDENTIFICATION

Chevy 10- and 12-bolt axle assemblies have been standard equipment on GM passenger cars, muscle cars, and trucks for decades. The rugged, reliable, and efficient Chevy 12-bolt has established itself as the preeminent rear differential for GM muscle cars since its debut in 1965. However, the smaller 10-bolt unfairly gained the reputation as a weak and inadequate rear end for high-performance applications. But there are several models in the 10-bolt line-up. The smaller 7.5- and 8.2-inch 10-bolt rear axles can't transmit horsepower loads in excess of 400 hp. However, the 8.5- and 8.6-inch 10-bolts are extremely stout and effective rear differentials that can transmit up to 1,000 hp to the rear wheels.

The GM 10-bolt rear end is quite possibly the most misunderstood and undervalued rear differential ever created. Even though it has been used in every major GM rear-wheel-drive platform, the 10-bolt has a bad reputation for being a low-performance unit. Nothing could be further from the truth. The 10-bolt can handle just about anything you throw at it, as long as you use the right axle, either the 8.5- or 8.6-inch. That is the great caveat; there are four sizes of 10-bolt GM rear ends: 7.5/7.625-, 8.2-, 8.5-, and 8.6-inch. These sizes refer to the diameter of the ring gear, and the one you use makes a big difference in the performance potential. The 8.5- and 8.6-inch provide superior performance and have a larger ring and pinion gear surface to handle high horsepower. Also, these surfaces run cooler because of their sheer size.

10-Bolt Identification

You need to be able to accurately identify the GM 10-bolt. Therefore, you need be able to choose the more desirable 8.5- or 8.6-inch and avoid the smaller 7.5/7.625- and 8.2-inch units. Identifying the 10-bolt axle is easy. The nomenclature actually refers to the number of ring gear bolts. The outer cover matches; 10 bolts hold the cover onto the housing.

This is the Moser Engineering 12-bolt axle assembly. As you can see, the Chevy 12-bolt differential is one stout axle, and it was the rear axle of choice for GM muscle cars and many GM competition cars. Big-block Chevelles, Camaros, and other GM high-performance vehicles were fitted with the 12-bolt limited-slip axle to maximize torque transfer and traction. (Photo Courtesy Moser Engineering)

This ring-and-pinion gear has suffered catastrophic failure. Be sure the mesh is correct and that the installed parts are correct so you don't destroy components. If you take off the center section cover and discover this kind of damage, you need to identify the cause so you don't repeat this type of failure.

8.2 Vehicle Applications

The 8.2 10-bolts are commonly found in the following vehicles.

Body	Years	Models
A-Body	1964–1972	Chevelle, Skylark, Cutlass, etc.
B-Body	1964–1972	Caprice, Biscayne, etc.
F-Body	1967–1970	Camaro, Firebird
X-Body	1964–1971	Chevy II, Nova, etc.

8.2-Inch Units

The key to identifying the 8.2 is the shape of the housing and the spacing between the lower bolts on the cover. The 8.2 has a smooth, round lower case area, with an 11-inch cover that has a diagonal indentation at the top or a 10⅝-inch irregular-shaped cover. The pinion nut should measure 1⅛ inches, as long as it is the OEM pinion nut.

Inside the 8.2, the ring gear bolts have 9/16-inch socket heads with 3/8-24 threads. The pinion diameter is 1.438 inches with 25 splines. The axles are retained by a set of C-clips on the inner end of the axle shaft inside the carrier.

8.5-Inch Units

Most 8.5-inch 10-bolts have two lugs on the bottom of the housing at the 5 and 7 o'clock positions. These should be square blocks, each with the outer side 90 degrees (vertical) to the road and the bottom-side surface horizontal to the road. The covers are often 11 inches round with a bulge on the driver's side for the ring gear or a 10⅝-inch irregular shape with the same bulge. The distance between the lower cover bolt and either adjacent bolt is 3¾ inches. The pinion nut is 1¼ inches.

The 8.5-inch differentials have 10¾-inch hex head bolts with 7/16-20-inch left-hand thread or reverse-thread bolts that hold the ring gear to the carrier. The pinion shaft diameter is 1.625 inches with 28 or 30 splines, which is the same as the GM 12-bolt design. Most 8.5 10-bolts are C-clip axles, so a set of C-clips retains the inner end of the axle shaft inside the carrier.

A variant of this axle assembly was used in 1971–1972 Buick GSs and Skylarks, Oldsmobile Cutlasses, and some 1969–1972 Pontiac Grand Prixs, as well as the 1970–1972 Monte

Buick and Oldsmobile bolt-in axles mount at the bearing flanges on the housing ends. They retain the axle shafts in the event of a failure. The four bolts that hold the drum back plate on also retain the flange. Note that this axle has been converted to disc brakes.

Bolt-in axles include (right to left) the axle, retainer plate, split washer shim, press-on bearing, and housing end. To remove the axle shafts, you need to remove the four bolts.

The rear cover's shape and the number of bolts are identifying features for GM rear differentials. The round 10-bolt cover with a bulge for the ring gear identifies this axle assembly as an 8.5-inch 10-bolt. The two lugs on the lower case at the 5 and 7 o'clock positions are also identifying features. The 8.2-inch differential does not have these lugs.

A pair of long flat areas on the front side of each axle tube is a clear indicator of an 8.5-inch Chevy 10-bolt.

8.5-inch Vehicle Applications

General Motors installed the 8.5 10-bolt axle assemblies in many of its most popular vehicles.

Body	Years	Models
A-Body	1970–1977	Chevelle, Skylark, Cutlass, etc.
B-Body	1970–1996	Caprice, Impala, Bel-Air, etc.
E-Body	1975–1978	Buick Riviera
F-Body	1970–1981	Camaro, Firebird Carlo, etc.
X-Body	1970–1979	Nova, Omega, etc.
N/A	1979–2008	Trucks/vans (includes 8.6)

To help you identify the 8.2-inch housing, remember that it may have an irregular-shaped cover or a round cover, but it does not have lugs as on the 8.5-inch.

Carlos. These axle assemblies had bolt-in axles and were used sporadically in A-Body wagons as well. These are highly sought after, and as such, are hard to find. In this version, the axles bolt to the housing ends just as on a Ford 8- or 9-inch. This means that in the event of an axle break, the wheel stays on the car.

7.5/7.625-Inch Units

To positively identify the Chevy 10-bolt in the 7.5/7.625-inch size, you need to measure it because it is very similar to the 8.5-inch housing. The case has a similar pair of lugs at the base of the center of the housing, which are located at 5 and 7 o'clock. However, the 7.5-inch lugs

7.5/7.6-Inch Vehicle Applications

General Motors installed the Chevy 10-bolt 7.5/7.6-inch differentials in the following vehicles.

Body	Years	Models
B-Body	1978–1996	Caprice, Oldsmobile 98, etc.
F-Body	1981–2002	Camaro and Firebird
G-Body	1977–1988	Malibu, Regal, Cutlass, El Camino, etc.
H-Body	1975–up GM	Vega and Monza
S-Series	1982–2005	Trucks and SUVs (4-cylinder)
N/A	1982–2005	GM mini-van, Astro, Safari

are smaller, with the outer side running at an angle and the inner side cut with a radius. The oval-shaped cover measures 8⅝₁₆ inches by 10⅝₁₆ inches. The distance between the lower center cover bolt and its adjacent bolts is 3¼ inches. Inside, the ring gear bolts are the same as the 8.5 corporate unit. However, the pinion shaft measures 1.438 inches. The axles are retained by a set of C-clips on the inner end of the axle shaft inside the carrier.

Chevy 10-Bolt Models

Although the 8.5- and 8.6-inch rear axles are more than capable of handling 400 hp (and with some setups a bit more), the 10-bolt name has a bad reputation due to the inherently weaker 7.5 and 8.2 designs. Because these two sizes are so common in pre-1971 (8.2) and 1975–2002 (7.5) vehicles, the 8.5 is lumped into the same group. This design was used in all GM rear-drive cars from 1964 through 1972. The 8.2 was phased out starting in 1971; it was replaced by the 8.5-inch "corporate" 10-bolt, and was installed in everything from Camaros and Chevelles until the mid-1980s. It remained in the 1/2-ton trucks until 1999, when the 8.6 replaced it, using the same basic design.

By far, the most common 10-bolt is the 7.5/7.6, and it has been around since 1975. It was installed on small trucks and vans up to the 2005 model year. There is very little aftermarket support for this axle assembly because it couldn't handle high-horsepower loads and therefore its performance potential was marginal. In street applications, the 7.5 is good for 350 to 400 hp with street tires and lots of wheel spin. When sticky traction bars and/or sticky tires

were installed, owners found that 400 hp can quickly turn the 7.5 into shrapnel.

In the final analysis, this axle is simply too small for high-horsepower cars, and so these axles should be avoided for most muscle cars and certainly any racing applications. Although gear sets and a locking differential are available, these are only suitable for a mild street engine or possibly a dirt track car. In the world of dirt track racing, some classes require a GM 7.5-inch 10-bolt and because there is no traction on dirt, this rear works very well.

Millions of 8.2-inch axle assemblies were built and many can be found in salvage yards. And like the 7.5 axle, it has a fair amount of aftermarket support but the ring gear is too small and therefore it cannot handle much torque. If installed on a 400-hp or stronger engine, it often fails. And unfortunately, there simply isn't enough room to install bigger axles, so it isn't a viable option for a high-performance car. To support high torque and horsepower loads, the axle shafts need a larger diameter and spline count. Combined with the small outer bearing races, the 8.2 is limited to 28-spline axles.

For performance vehicles, the 8.2 can typically handle up to 400 hp with street tires, but that's the limit for this axle. If you bolt on even a set of drag radials, the axles bend or break, along with having the potential for breaking the gears and carrier themselves. You can build these for performance, but if you use sticky tires, the superior traction and consequent strain from the grip will kill it quickly on the drag strip.

There are temporary fixes for the 8.2, such as a carrier girdle, but they don't provide a reliable and suitably

strong solution. When too much torque or traction is fed through the axle, it will eventually break the axle.

The 8.5- and 8.6-inch 10-bolts have larger ring-and-pinion gears, which makes an important difference. These rear axle assemblies can handle up to 400 hp. Among the Chevy 10-bolt family of axles, these provide the best performance and durability. The car versions were in production from 1971 to 1987. General Motors has been using this axle assembly in cars for 16 years and in 1/2-ton trucks for 30 years. The 2010-up Camaro uses a similar design (8.6 10-bolt) in the center section of its independent rear suspension.

The 8.5 is limited to 30-spline axles, but can withstand 1,000 hp with slicks when properly built. The factory installed the 8.5-inch 10-bolt in the Buick Grand National, and that's the biggest claim to fame for this OEM axle. In stock form, the 8.5 can support wheel-standing launches from the turbocharged 6-cylinder. At just 3/8-inch smaller than the 8.875-inch 12-bolt differential, the 8.5-inch ring gear is strong enough for high-performance applications.

The aftermarket fully supports the 8.5. Gears of all sizes, limited-slip or Posi-Traction, lockers, and spools are offered. Affordable performance is what the 8.5 is all about. Considering the challenges of the typical 12-bolt swap for most muscle cars, when the 10-bolt units are often a bolt-in swap, the 8.5 10-bolt starts to look really good.

10-Bolt Carriers

Several differential carriers are offered for the 10-bolt axle assemblies. However, only certain gear sets are offered for the carriers, especially

---

10-Bolt Carrier Codes

Carriers are coded for their particular series. The most common numbers are as follows.

Axle Type	Series	ID Code	Gear Ratio
8.2	2-Series	ED32118	2.73:1 and lower
8.2	3-Series	EDB30116	3.08:1 and higher
8.5	2-Series	410409N	2.56:1 and lower
8.5	3-Series	410408N	2.73:1 and higher

if you change gear ratios. Typically, 10-bolt carriers are specific to a series of gears. A 2-Series carrier holds 2.56:1 and higher gears (numerically lower) such as 2.41. These are very high gears, good for top speed, not for off-the-line performance. The 3-Series carriers are good for 2.73 and lower gears, so 3.08 and 3.73 gears work well.

Most axle assemblies have open differentials. The open differential does not have anything in the middle of the carrier between the side gears. If this were a limited-slip or Posi-Traction differential, you would see the clutch packs in the middle of the carrier and between the side gears.

In this photo, you clearly see the clutch packs with springs, so indeed these are limited-slip differentials. A Yukon aftermarket clutch-type limited-slip differential is on the left; the GM Posi-Traction differential from a 1971 Buick Gran Sport 8.5 10-bolt is on the right. As you can see, the Yukon casting is much thicker and so are the springs.

The stock axles for both Chevy 10- and 12-bolt differentials use C-clips unless you have one of the rare bolt-in axle units. A small bolt in the center of the carrier retains the crossbar.

The C-clips are not the strongest method for retaining the axle shafts; many owners convert the Chevy 10- and 12-bolt axles to a flange type, which retains the axle if it fails. To remove the C-clip, you push the axle in to allow room to snag the C-clip with a pick. Once the C-clip has been removed, the axle slides out of the housing.

The placement of the casting numbers on an 8.2-inch 10-bolt varies by year and model. When you decode these numbers you can conclusively identify your axle.

Engine torque and suspension loads are placed on the rear axle assemblies, which are also subjected to moisture, dirt, and anything the road can throw at it. You may need to clean the rear housing before you can decode the casting numbers. You can simply clean the area around the casting pad, but a power washer and some hot soapy water can work wonders for 40 years of grime.

10-Bolt Housings by the Numbers

Before you rebuild any axle, you should identify which axle you have. Once you have identified the housing, you must order the correct parts for the particular axle. The casting numbers for 10-bolt rear differentials are typically located either on the forward side of the passenger-side axle tube or on the driver's side. These numbers are approximately 3 inches from the center section.

The two examples at right show you how to decode 10-bolt housings.

1970 axle code: COZ 01 01 G E

COZ	Ratio
01	Month
01	Day of month
G	Plant
E	Posi-Traction source

1971+ rear axle code: CB G 112 1 E

CB	Ratio
G	Plant
112	Day of year
1	Shift
E	Posi-Traction source

10-Bolt Gears by the Numbers

Gears are also "coded" with their teeth count; dividing the number of ring gear teeth by the number of the pinion gear teeth yields the ratio.

10-Bolt Assembly Plant Codes

Code*	Plant	Code*	Plant
B	Buick	O	Oldsmobile
C	Buffalo	P	Pontiac
D	Cadillac	M	Pontiac/Canada
G	Detroit Gear & Axle	W	Warren, MI
K	GM of Canada		

* You may also see a shift number, in which 1 is the day shift and 2 is the night shift.

10-Bolt Gear Codes

Axle Ratio (:1)	Ring Gear Tooth Count	Pinion Gear Tooth Count	Axle Ratio (:1)	Ring Gear Tooth Count	Pinion Gear Tooth Count
2.56	41	16	3.36	37	11
2.73	41	15	3.42	41	12
3.07	43	14	3.55	39	11
3.08	40	13	3.73	41	11
3.08	37	12	4.10	41	10
3.31	43	13	4.11	37	9

10-Bolt Posi-Traction Source Codes

Code	Source
D	Dana Posi-Traction Differential
E	Eaton Posi-Traction Differential
G	Chevrolet G&A Posi-Traction Carrier
O	Oldsmobile Posi-Traction Carrier
W	Warren/Warner Motive
–	No Posi-Traction

A full range of pinion gears is offered for the Chevy 10- and 12-bolt axle assemblies so you are able to select the correct gear set for your vehicle, application, and setup. These are two pinion gears for the 8.5-inch 10-bolt. The pinion on the left is part of a 4.11:1 gear set; the one on the right is a 3.08:1 pinion. You can see the dramatic difference in not only teeth but in overall diameter.

The tooth count is stamped on the head of each pinion for both the pinion and the ring gear. As you can see, 13 is the hypoid gear count for the pinion and 40 is the ring gear count. Pinion gears and ring gears are not interchangeable because they are designed for the specific (correct) mesh. Therefore, the specified pinion and ring gears must be used together.

Limited-Slip versus Open Differentials

As you may know, GM's product name for a limited-slip differential is Posi-Traction. Most GM muscle car owners choose to install or use an axle assembly with Posi-Traction because it provides superior traction and performance compared to an open differential. A limited-slip differential senses wheel slip and directs torque to the wheel that is not slipping, so acceleration is optimized.

Two methods are used to determine if an axle has a limited-slip differential. A strong but not definitive indication that axle assembly has (or once had) Posi-Traction from the factory is a metal tag on one of the rear cover bolts that reads, "Use Limited Slip Lube Only."

However, a hands-on mechanical test of the differential is the only certain way to determine if it is indeed a limited-slip. First, you must raise the rear of the vehicle and place the vehicle on jackstands. Set the transmission in neutral. Grab one wheel and spin it while having a helper watch the other wheel. A correctly functioning limited-slip differential spins both tires in the same direction. An open differential spins the other wheel in the opposite direction.

Although this hands-on test provides a good indication, it is not conclusive because a badly abused differential with worn clutches can function like an open carrier. ∎

12-Bolt Identification

When it comes to GM muscle cars and sports cars, the 12-bolt axle has been the top high-performance axle assembly for decades. Compared to the Ford 9-inch, the 12-bolt positions the pinion gear higher on the ring gear. This reduces the load on the pinion, resulting in less parasitic loss from the friction and load.

The 12-bolt was introduced in 1964 and installed in cars and trucks until 1972. From 1972-on, General Motors installed its 10-bolt in cars and it remained an option for trucks until 1987.

This 1967 Chevy truck used a trailing-arm design with coil and leaf springs. The half-leaf spring (left) serves as an overload spring for heavy loads or trailering.

Unlike the various 10-bolts, the 12-bolt axle assembly has different components for cars and trucks. The passenger car 12-bolt has an oval-shaped differential cover, and it measures 10^{15}/₁₆ x 10⅝ inches.

Trucks have a smaller inner pinion shaft (1.438 inches versus 1.675 inches) and bearing, and the pinion rides lower on the ring gear. In addition, the truck 12-bolt has an irregular shape. The early truck 12-bolts had large axle splines with only 12 splines. The differential carriers are also narrower than on the passenger car units, and they do not interchange. That does not mean

General Motors installed different axles for different applications. Axles for high-performance or heavy-duty applications commonly used higher spline-count axles while common passenger car axles use lower spline counts. The top axle is an 8.5-inch 10-bolt with 30 splines; the bottom axle is an 8.5-inch with 28 splines. Note the thicker head on the bottom axle where the C-clip rides. This is specific to the carrier. The carrier and axles must match.

General Motors used several different suspension designs in their passenger cars throughout the 1960s and 1970s. This 8.5-inch 10-bolt came from a 1971 Buick GS. The large bushings at the top of the differential housing connect to the triangulated four-bar trailing arm system that the Buick used. It is more difficult to swap these housings from car to car if they do not share the same suspension design.

that the truck units are not capable of performance builds because aftermarket 30-spline carriers and axles are available.

The truck 12-bolt axles are much more affordable than the car units because they are more plentiful but these units have fewer splines so they are not as strong as the axle in the car assemblies. In addition, the trucks typically have larger axles and brakes.

Most passenger car 12-bolts used a four-bar trailing arm mounting system, with the exception of the Camaro and Nova, which used leaf springs. GM trucks from 1961 through 1967 used a two-bar trailing arm mount, while the 1968-up trucks used leaf springs. There is some crossover on the trucks, as some earlier trucks had leaves and some later trucks had the trailing arms.

All GM 12-bolts use C-clip–style axles. Aftermarket 12-bolt housings are based on the passenger car design.

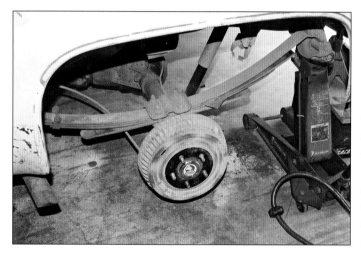

Camaros, Novas, and 1968 and later trucks used leaf springs like these. The axle may be over or under the leaf, depending on the application.

C2 and C3 Corvettes (built from 1963 to 1981) used a non-standard 10-bolt design. They used an independent rear suspension with transverse leaf springs. As a result, these cars use a specialized axle housing for this suspension, and it's not easily upgraded. You need to machine the housing to accept a 12-bolt carrier, which also requires custom axles. Essentially, the housing is machined to clear the larger gears and carrier, and it's not a job for the novice.

12-Bolt Vehicle Applications

General Motors installed the 12-bolt rear end in several passenger cars.

Body	Years	Models
A-Body	1964–1972	Chevelle, Cutlass, GTO
B-body	1964–1972	Caprice, Impala
F-Body	1967–1972	Camaro, Firebird
X-Body	1964–1972	Chevy II, Nova

12-Bolt Gear Codes

The following is a list for the factory gear sizes available for each series of the passenger car 12-bolt.

2-Series
Gear Ratio (:1)	Ring Gear Tooth Count	Pinion Gear Tooth Count
2.29	32	14
2.56	41	16
2.73	41	15

3-Series
Gear Ratio (:1)	Ring Gear Tooth Count	Pinion Gear Tooth Count
3.07	43	14
3.31	43	13
3.55	39	11
3.73	41	11

4-Series
Gear Ratio (:1)	Ring Gear Tooth Count	Pinion Gear Tooth Count
4.10	41	10
4.56	41	9
4.88	39	8

12-Bolt Carriers

The 12-bolt carriers also use the same series-specific system as do the 10-bolts; each carrier only works with certain gear sizes. The types are 2-, 3-, and 4-Series. The 2-Series is by far the most common.

12-Bolt Housings by the Numbers

The casting numbers for the 12-bolt housings are typically found on the upper rear of the driver's side of the center section. The casting numbers are simple to decode.

The first letter is the month of the year; A is January, B is February, and so on. The next digit is the day it was built, and the last digit is the year it was built. For example, a 12-bolt axle that was built on March 28, 1967, is C287.

On the passenger-side front tube, the stamped axle code designates either 1969-and-earlier units or 1969-and-later builds. The 1969-and-earlier codes have two letters, then a four-digit number, followed by a letter, and possibly a shift number, for which 1 is the day shift and 2 is the night shift.

And finally, a Posi-Traction number was used.

For 1969 and later, the code typically features six to eight digits, including three letters, three numbers, and sometimes an additional number and letter. The first two letters indicate the gear-ratio code, the third letter notes the build plant, and three numbers designate the build day from 001 to 365. Sometimes the shift code is stamped, and if the unit has a Posi-Traction, you see a P stamp.

The Chevy 12-bolt axle assemblies for passenger cars feature an oval cover with a diagonal indentation. This is a 1969 Chevelle 12-bolt housing.

Truck 12-bolts have an irregular cover with a ring gear pocket. This example is a 1967 Chevy C10. The truck housings are not as durable as the passenger car housings due to a narrower carrier and a smaller inner pinion bearing.

12-Bolt Axle Ratio Codes

Axle Code	Axle Ratio (:1)	Axle Type	Axle Code	Axle Ratio (:1)	Axle Type
CA	3.08		FM	3.36	Posi-Traction
CB	3.36		FN	3.55	
CC	3.73		FO	3.55	Posi-Traction
CD	3.07	Posi-Traction	FP	3.70	
CE	3.08	Posi-Traction	K2	3.55	
CF	3.31	Posi-Traction	K3	3.55	Posi-Traction
CG	3.36	Posi-Traction	K4	3.73	
CH	2.73	Posi-Traction	K5	3.73	Posi-Traction
CI	3.73	Posi-Traction	K6	4.10	Posi-Traction
CJ	3.08		K7	4.56	Posi-Traction
CP	2.73		K8	4.88	Posi-Traction
CR	3.70	Posi-Traction	KA	3.55	
CU	3.73	Posi-Traction with metallic brakes	KB	3.55	Posi-Traction
			KC	2.73	Posi-Traction
CV	3.70		KD	2.73	
CW	3.31		KF	3.55	Posi-Traction
CX	3.07		KJ	3.55	
CY	3.07		KK	4.10	Posi-Traction
CZ	2.73		KM	4.56	Posi-Traction
FH	2.73		KO	4.88	Posi-Traction
FI	2.73	Posi-Traction	KW	2.73	With metallic brakes
FJ	3.08				
FK	3.08	Posi-Traction	KX	3.07	Posi-Traction
FL	3.36		KY	3.31	Posi-Traction
			KZ	3.31	

12-Bolt Assembly Plant Codes

Code	Location
B	Buffalo, New York
G	Chevrolet Gear & Axle
W	Warren, Michigan
K	McKinnon Industries

12-Bolt Production Month Codes

Code	Month
01	January
02	February
03	March
04	April
05	May
06	June
07	July
08	August
09	September
10	October
11	November
12	December

SUSPENSION TYPES AND DIFFERENTIAL HOUSINGS

General Motors has been using variations of the 10- and 12-bolt differential since the mid-1960s so many different housings are in use. The basic 10-bolt has been used in every type of vehicle, for both rear and front (four-wheel drive) applications. The 12-bolt passenger car design was relatively short lived,

with an eight-year run, but the truck version ran through the late 1980s, so many vehicles use those.

GM differential housings have used several types of mounting styles, including leaf springs, coil springs with trailing arms, coil springs with a triangulated four-link, and independent rear suspension (IRS). Front

differentials are either leaf springs or independent front suspension (IFS). Some housings can be converted to another suspension system while others cannot; it just depends on the design of the suspension, particularly in the case of four-link rear systems. You can adapt a four-link housing to a leaf spring car, but it requires so much fabrication that it is not practical to install a leaf spring housing to a four-link.

Leaf Spring Rear Suspension

A leaf spring mounting system uses a pair of arched steel or fiberglass leaf packs to suspend the rear housing from the frame. The leaf packs are typically made up of multiple leaves, but in some cases, these are single-leaf springs. The leaves use two mounting points to the chassis in the front and rear of the housing itself.

The housing may be mounted above or below the leaf springs. The housing is below the springs in most trucks for added ride height, and is called overslung. The housing is typically underslung, or mounted below

To start the disassembly of the differential, first you remove the center cover. You can clearly see the ring gear and carrier, which contains the limited-slip clutch pack. In a typical high-mileage rebuild, you need to replace most of the bearings, gaskets, and seals.

The leaf spring rear suspension is fitted to Camaros, Novas, trucks, and several other vehicles. This leaf spring Chevy truck has an overslung housing (the housing is positioned underneath the springs).

Older pre-1968 Chevy and GMC trucks have a long trailing-arm setup like this. They used a large coil spring. For heavy loads a half-leaf overload spring was optional.

Installing traction bars is an effective fix for wheel hop. They bolt to the housing mount under the leaf pack and extend forward to the front leaf spring mount. As the housing tries to rotate upward on heavy acceleration, the bar contacts the front mount, locking the leaf spring in shape so that it can't wrap, and thereby eliminating the effect of wheel hop. Different versions of these devices are available, but the principle is the same with each.

Watt's Linkage Rear Suspension

When torque is applied to a leaf spring suspension design, it has a tendency to walk from side to side. This is due to the rubber bushings, the way the rear of the springs are mounted with two hanging shackles, and the multiple leaves. Leaf spring suspensions have certain drawbacks. When a leaf spring car enters a corner, the entire leaf pack compresses and can fan out slightly, just like a deck of cards.

In addition, leaf spring shackles and bushings can flex so suspension actuation is sloppy. As a result, handling deteriorates and it becomes difficult to negotiate corners at higher speeds.

One of the better solutions for this problem is a Watt's linkage, which connects both sides' leaf packs with an articulating arm in the center to keep the housing from wandering from side to side under heavy loads. These work extremely well and are often used in road race vehicles.

Originally designed by James Watt in 1784, the linkage was intended for the Watt steam engine. Also referred to as parallel motion, the Watt's linkage prevents side-to-side movement

the spring pack, in most passenger cars, and lowers the ride height.

Leaf springs can suffer from axle wrap. Under heavy acceleration, the rear springs twist up against the forward rotation of the tires. As the housing rotates, the leaf springs contort against their natural arch. The front of the leaf rises and allows the housing to rotate. When the leaf spring cannot wrap any more, it snaps back into its natural state and shocks the tires. Unfortunately, this often happens several times. Once the wrap and

snap has occurred, it tends to become a cycle. The rear wheels jump up and down and the rear of the vehicle starts bouncing up and down. Hence you get the term: "wheel hop." This results in a dangerous loss of control and so it must be remedied.

Trucks are more susceptible to this condition because beds are light and do not place much weight on the axle unless there is something in the bed. If you punch the gas and the back end starts hopping, you have to let up on the gas to stop it.

by providing a solid location at the center of the vehicle. The propeller is mounted in the center of the vehicle on a bracket that is attached to the chassis. The two side arms connect to the propeller, which rotates as the suspension moves up and down. This allows free vertical movement, but positively locates the housing in the center of the car.

Coil Spring Rear Suspension

This is the more versatile form of rear suspension because it provides a lot of tuning latitude. A coil spring is not susceptible to axle wrap because every coil spring rear suspension uses solid bars to connect the housing to the chassis. Two main types of factory links are used with 10- and 12-bolt designs: trailing arms and the triangulated four-link.

Trailing Arm Axle

A trailing arm is a long bar that runs from the forward portion of the chassis to the rear where the housing is mounted. Trailing arms are typically used in an underslung axle assembly. Trailing arm axles are commonly found on GMC and Chevy trucks built from 1960 through 1968.

This design works well because the trailing arms are quite long. Their front pivot point is in the center of the chassis, so it yields excellent handling characteristics. The drawback for this design is that coil springs simply cannot handle extreme loads.

For this reason, coil springs are not often used for the rear suspension of trucks. The factory fix was a half-leaf overload spring, but that did not solve the tramping, or wheel-hop, conditions until they converted to a leaf pack in the late 1960s.

Passenger cars from the early 1960s often had the trailing arm design too, including the GM X-frame B-Body cars (Impala, Biscayne, etc.), but these cars don't have 10- or 12-bolt differentials.

The coil spring in most trailing arm designs is positioned on the trailing arm itself, so it connects to a spring pad on the frame. This can make for some awkward spring angles on the car versions, but trucks use longer springs that sit vertical. One of the nicer aspects of working on a trailing arm vehicle with the spring on the arm is that you don't have to disconnect the suspension to remove the housing.

Panhard Bar Axle

The panhard bar is a long bar that connects one side of the housing to the opposite side of the chassis with only two bars and one chassis mount per bar. The trailing arm design needs to locate the housing to the center of the chassis, and the panhard bar connects to the housing in the center of the chassis. In stock form, this bar is solid and not adjustable. Adjustable upgrades are available from the aftermarket.

With a panhard bar, the vertical motion of the axle is more controlled; however, it swings to one side in a slight arc. This is due to the fact that the bar cannot change length; the housing must move along this arc to facilitate the vertical movement.

The longer the bar, the shallower the arc; therefore the less the side movement. Because of this, a panhard bar is much less effective on passenger cars than trucks. The bar is too short to effectively control the horizontal location and keep the tires from contacting the fender wells. General Motors installed these

Some 1960s and 1970s GM cars are not equipped with the common Chevy 10- or 12-bolt axle assemblies. This means that you need to positively identify the axle assembly before you begin work. The GM B-Body cars, such as the Impala and Caprice, used a version of the four-link system, but it is a little more complicated than the A- and G-Body versions. This 1962 Buick used an odd-ball differential that's unrelated to the 10 or 12-bolt, but the suspension is the same. This one uses a panhard bar as well.

bars on many of its cars in the early 1960s, and they have lots of space between the tires and the wheel lips because of it.

In addition, you cannot correct the suspension geometry and reduce the arc of travel. The only way to do that is to remove the panhard bar and convert to a Watt's linkage design.

Triangulated Four-Link Rear Suspension

When the muscle car era began, General Motors introduced its rear suspension version: the triangulated four-link. This design incorporates a pair of lower bars that run in-line with the chassis, and two very short upper arms that angle toward the center of the car at the top of the chassis. All four bars connect to different points on the housing. The lowers are on one plane while the uppers are on another plane. The goal is to maintain a singular vertical range of motion. It's also designed to

When a Chevy 10- or 12-bolt is pulled from a vehicle, it often looks like this but it may be even more greasy, grimy, and possibly rusty. Years of road grime pile up on the differential housing. So the first step is to strip it all away. The most common way to clean it is with a liberal coating of oven cleaner or engine degreaser, and then power wash it. If the axle housing is particularly rusty, you may need to media blast it after your initial degreasing.

eliminate the possibility of the housing wrapping up under acceleration and to reduce side-to-side deflection with the angled upper bars.

It's about the best factory suspension there is. The aftermarket equivalent is virtually identical in nature, and the triangulated upper bars are what set it apart from all the rest. These bars resist side-to-side movement because of the inward angle. This design eliminates the need for a panhard bar to keep the axle assembly from wandering side to side. However, this does not mean it is without fault.

In stock form, the bars with simple U-shaped channels can bend and twist under extreme use. Although the large rubber bushings provide an excellent ride, they are too soft and spongy for high-performance driving. Aftermarket upgrades include polyurethane bushings or even bearing conversions, and adjustable upper arms allow tuning of the pinion angle. Solid or tubular lower bars are another popular upgrade. The factory bars can be upgraded on the

The type of Chevy 10- and 12-bolt axle housing depends on the style of suspension. This GM A-Body frame uses the triangulated four-link system, so this housing fits only a GM A-Body car with this four-link system. This frame is also used on GM G-Body cars, though it is not a direct swap.

The axle housings for four-link suspensions have these upper bushings; this type of suspension is found on A- and G-Body cars. There is no easy way to remove these bushings and after years of use they are often worn or damaged. The best method is to use an air impact hammer and a chisel to crush the bushing end and then drive it out.

Once you have thoroughly cleaned the axle assembly, you should protect the surfaces. If you have stripped it down to the metal, it starts collecting surface rust immediately. So, it's a good idea to paint the axle assembly to prevent rust from forming and to make it look fresh. A new coat of paint makes a housing look much better than a crusty, greasy one. If you're not set up to paint it, you should coat it with WD-40 or some other lubricant to prevent rust from forming.

cheap by boxing them in. A plate is added to the open side of the channel, reinforcing the bars so that they do not bend or flex.

The springs are typically mounted to the housing for four-link suspensions, which makes removing them quite easy. The upper mounts are cast into the center section of the housing, which is a problem if you are looking to upgrade to a 12-bolt unit. You can't just weld mounts to the housing as you can with a leaf spring or trailing arm unit. Instead, you need to find either a factory 12-bolt housing or purchase an aftermarket version.

Independent Rear Suspension

The Corvette is the only regular production vehicle General Motors made that carried independent rear suspension. The 1963 through 1978 Corvettes were fitted with axles similar to the 10- and 12-bolt, but not exactly the same. However, conversions are available that use 12-bolt differentials in the C2 and C3 Corvette housing. Although a solid axle system is used in conjunction with a multi-link and leaf spring suspension system, an IRS system uses an independent axle shaft on each side, so both rear wheels can move independently according to road conditions and load on the suspension. The Corvette design, however, uses a transverse-mounted fiberglass mono-leaf spring, and that connects both sides of the axle.

Project: Building a Universal Axle

A universal axle is an indispensable tool when fitting a rear axle assembly to a vehicle (and it has several other uses). If you build many project cars and need to move them around, this is a good tool for you. How often do you wish you had a rolling axle that is adjustable for width and fits under anything? Although your initial answer may be "never," you might be surprised just how often this rig comes in handy, especially if you buy/build a lot of project cars. This universal axle can be used as a custom rear-end jig, trailering axle, and car body mover.

I first discovered the universal axle during a drag car build. My axle builder, Harold Evans of Perkins, Oklahoma, designed and built this adjustable axle so we could set up the rear of the drag car to fit with the wheel and tire combo, and he used it as a jig to build the narrowed housing. With that accomplished, I have this heavy-duty axle that expands from 45-inch to 65-inch with the turn of a couple bolts, and it has multiple bolt patterns for whatever wheels are needed.

You need a few spare parts for this project. I used pieces from a mid-1960s Chevy truck, but you can use whatever you have available. If you have to buy the parts, they are typically available on Craigslist or at a salvage yard. Drum-brake front spindles are easy to find and super cheap.

Here is the basic parts list:

- Drum brake spindles and hubs: Bolt pattern only matters if you are setting it up to use a specific wheel. I drilled mine for 5-on-4.75-inch, the most common GM pattern, plus I left the six-bolt pattern.
- Square tubing: You need two sizes. One is for the outer section and one is for the sliding inner section. I used 3-inch mild steel for the outer and 2.5-inch mild steel for the inner. The tubing was about 1/4-inch thick, strong enough to hold up the back end of a car.
- A good welder and the ability to cut the tubing square. If you don't have a metal bandsaw, you can have the steel shop cut it to size for you.
- Four nuts and bolts: A couple pairs of 1/2-inch nuts with 2-inch-long bolts lock the width of the axle.

The project is not complicated or extremely labor intensive so you can probably build it in a day. My machinist went the extra mile by fly-cutting the spindles on a lathe, but that is not absolutely necessary. Once you have one of these adjustable axles, you will find all kinds uses for it.

1 Wheel and Axle Fitment on Chassis

This project installs a tubular A-Body suspension. First, you need to build a dummy axle for suspension and axle fitment purposes. I used a set of drum spindles from a 1960s Chevy truck that had been converted to discs. You can also use late-model 4x4 front hubs, mid-1990s on up half-ton trucks work great. You can check with local shops for late-model 4x4 front hubs because they are frequently replaced. The bearings don't have to be in great shape for this tool.

2 Disassemble Drum Brakes

You disassemble the drum brakes to create the tool. Rivets often hold the drums to the hub; drill them out. I removed the cotter pin and castle nut that holds the rotor and hub on the spindle.

3 Remove Retention Bolts

With the drum and rotor removed, the bolts holding the steering arms can be accessed. Use a socket and ratchet or wrench to remove the retention bolts.

4 Remove Steering Arm

Once the steering arm has been removed, the bolts can come out. The steering arm is held on with two fine-thread nuts and bolts.

5 Remove Splash Shield

Sometimes the splash shields and bearings are difficult to remove, so I set the splash shield on the bench and smacked the shaft with a hammer. I positioned a length of steel stock on the end of the spindle and gave it some firm taps with a dead-blow hammer. If you need to use a hammer, protect the spindle threads. If you damage the threads, the castle nut won't thread back on.

6 Remove Cover

To separate the cover from the hub, you need to drill out the rivets on the cover. If necessary, use a punch and a hammer to knock them out.

7 Cut Bracket Off Spindle

Once the cover has been removed and the spindle has been separated, you can cut the bracket off the spindle because you only need the spindle and the rotor to perform this procedure.

8 Cut Off Bracket

To make the tool easier to use, you can cut off the bracket. Most mechanics use a reciprocating saw. In this case, the machinist used a band saw to cut off the top half of the spindle.

9 Clean Up Spindle

The backside of the spindles need to be flat to weld the spindle to the square steel tube. In addition, the width of each spindle should be the same so the measuring and fitment process is easier. You can use an angle grinder to clean up the spindle. One of the benefits to being in a machine shop is that the machinist can turn down the back of the spindle in a metal lathe for a flush fit.

10 Inspect Spindle

Your spindle should look similar to this. You want the back of the spindle to have enough surface area to easily weld it to the dummy axle. With a lathe, it only took about four minutes to do this portion.

11 Position Spindle Against Tubing

Position the spindle flush against the 3-inch square tubing; the spindle needs to be square against this tube to achieve accurate measurements. The spindle needs to be accurately machined flat. If the axle is for sizing custom rear differential housings, the wheel needs to roll true and not wobble.

12 Weld Spindle to Axle Tube

You can use a MIG welder to weld the top and bottom of the spindle to the square axle tube.

13 Inspect Axle Tube

The dummy axle tube has an extendable end tube on one side so it can be used for mocking up the axle width on different vehicles. It slides over the end and four bolts tighten to hold it in place. The center section is made of a section of 2.5-inch tubing welded inside one half of the 3-inch tubing.

14 Inspect Axle Tube (CONTINUED)

These bolts lock the extendable tube into the proper position so accurate sizing can be attained.

15 Drill and Tap Rotors

Drill and tap the rotors for the 5-on-4.75-inch bolt pattern. Use a set of bolts, rather than studs because studs would limit you to one bolt pattern. This axle was put to use in a drag car, setting up the rear suspension and width for the custom housing.

16 Roll Dummy Axle Under Car

Install the wheels on the hubs and roll the dummy axle assembly under the car. At this stage, you can precisely measure width and take several height measurements. The key measurements are ride height, overall width, space between the tires and inner fenders and outer fenders, as well as squareness in the chassis. With accurate ride height and width measurements, you can order the correct rear housing for this project. After this project, you can also use the axle to move a project car whose rear differential has been previously liberated from the chassis.

17 Measure Ride Height

Use a level and tape measure to measure the desired ride height for the car. You are looking for about 8 inches of space between the axle centerline and the top of the wheel arch. Both sides need to match. This helps determine the correct width and clearance for the new rear-end housing.

Front Suspension

Two types of suspension can be found up front: leaf or IFS. You can certainly swap the front housing for either one, but the 10-bolt version was only used in leaf spring trucks.

Just as with the rear leaf design, the front leaf in trucks is oversprung, so it's easy to add clearance with a block lift. At the place where the axles come out of the ends, steering knuckles on the front housing connect to the wheel hub though a U-joint. The axle itself has a yoke on the end that holds one side of the U-joint, and the wheel hub connects to the other. This allows the steering knuckle to articulate. Newer four-wheel-drive trucks use constant velocity (CV) joints instead for longer life.

The 8.5-inch 10-bolt front axles were used from 1977 through 1991. When the GM 8.25-inch differential was introduced, the company used a completely different independent front suspension design. GM trucks with IFS use a design that is not similar to the 10- and 12-bolt differential.

Advanced Suspension Components

On classic GM cars and trucks, the rear suspension cradles the Chevy 10- or 12-bolt axle assembly and therefore, it plays a pivotal role in application of power to the ground as do the components inside the housing itself. To restore the original ride and handling, you can simply replace the stock bushings with rubber or poly-graphite bushings. But vintage muscle cars have antiquated handling and suspension performance. Even some modern compact cars can corner better than most of our preferred classic muscle. If you want to carve corners and put more power to the ground, a more substantial change is necessary. Many aftermarket companies offer suspension solutions, including Heigts, Chassisworks, Art Morrison, and Detroit Speed for classic GM rear-wheel-drive cars.

Global West Systems

Global West offers two lines of advanced suspension components: the Negative Roll and G-Plus. The Negative Roll system is the more advanced of the two. It requires tall spindles and delivers superior performance. But it is designed for road race applications and can be a little harsh on the street.

For most street-driven applications, the G-Plus system is the better option, offering performance and versatility in one complete kit. The G-Plus system can be used with stock, 2-inch-drop, or ATS spindles. It also works with most stock-style spindles, so almost any braking system can be used. I opted for a Global West system for the Buick. This kit includes the choice of using coil springs or coil-over shocks. Although the Global West coil springs are certainly capable of a quality ride,

I opted for the adjustability and control of the coil-over shocks. Global West uses QA-1 shocks with coil-over springs exclusively. Many consider these to be the best in the industry. I selected the double-adjustable shocks, which have 24 settings each for rebound and compression. These shocks offer 576 tuning options, which might seem intimidating at first, but after becoming familiar with the settings, they are easy to use and adjust.

I initially set up the system with all four shocks in the middle at 12 clicks. The car rode somewhat firm, but it certainly felt as if I were in control. I wanted a low ride height to accentuate the new Centerline Retro 17-inch billet wheels and Kumho Ecsta Supra rubber that provides the grip. The benefit of coil-overs is that you can run them high, low, or anywhere in between, so they're the perfect solution for any performance ride.

My setup placed the 24.5-inch-tall tires about 1-inch from the inner fender, and as a result, there would never be enough clearance with a stock system. However, I had enough clearance and therefore no tire rubbing issues with the Global West kit with the exception of at the very end of the testing. During the final stint, I had the steering locked and suspension in full tilt; only a little rubbing occurred.

Sway Bar Upgrade

The 1971 Buick GS was going to be subjected to higher cornering speeds so a sway bar upgrade was in order. I installed an Addco 1⅛-inch front and a 1-inch rear sway bar. Global West also offers factory-size sway bars, making it a simple package purchase. A common mistake when choosing sway bars is to go too large. A sway bar that's larger than necessary creates more handling problems than it solves. It pulls the inside tire off the ground in a hard corner. Corner entry understeer and corner exit oversteer are just a couple of the problems caused by using sway bars that are too big. Global West does not suggest using a 1¼-inch sway bar with their suspension systems for the GM A-body.

The installation is quite simple and it took less than a weekend to complete. Fitting new components requires more than one set of hands and helpers always make things go a little faster. You need a few tools: a pickle fork to remove the ball joints and an impact gun to remove rusted nuts and bolts.

Handling Improvement

All of the modifications dramatically improve the handling of the car. Not only is cornering improved, but straight-line performance and braking are improved as well. To quantify the improvements, I performed some skid-pad testing using a Vericom VC3000 testing computer.

This computer uses horizontal and lateral accelerometers to measure G-forces and complex formulas to calculate the results. The Vericom is the most accurate data-logging computer of its kind, and the company kindly loaned one to me.

To perform a skid pad test, the car is driven in a large circle, at a steady pace. As each round is completed, the circle is turned tighter and tighter as well as faster and faster. As soon as the rear tires begin to slip, the G-forces are recorded. This is the amount of lateral force that a suspension can handle.

In stock form, the GS recorded .671 G on the skid pad, which is certainly respectable handling. With the G-Plus suspension installed (very little setup was required), the Buick GS convertible pulled 1.04 Gs, which was a vast improvement. At 1 G, you really feel the cornering forces

and it was very difficult to make the rear slide under consistent power. Of course, with more than 400 horses on tap, a quick mash of the pedal would certainly get things hairy pretty quickly.

Under hard cornering, the GS now sticks hard to the road and feels like it's on rails. The steering is tighter with the improved geometry. The bumps that used to send me bouncing out of the seat are now handled with ease, quite surprising considering the extremely low stance I set for the coil-over springs.

Once the car is done, I plan on hitting a couple of open-track days to see how capable the GS really is. Until then, the back roads will just have to do.

Project: Installing an A-Body Axle with Tubular Arms

Stock control arms (top) are made of stamped steel and they flex and deflect, changing the geometry of the suspension when under load. The aftermarket tubular control arms (bottom) are made of high-strength steel alloy; but more important, the tubular design provides much greater strength over the stock control arms. In addition, the tubular arms afford adjustability to the suspension for particular street or competition conditions. The uppers are adjusted to match the factory length.

1 Inspect Control Arm

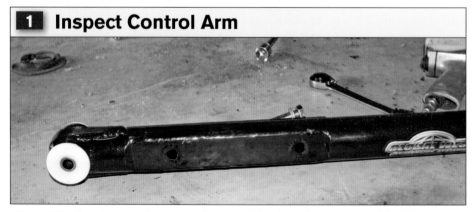

Global West makes control arms for a variety of makes and models. They are far stronger and provide far better suspension performance than the stock stamped steel arms. The lower arms (shown) feature Delrin bushings and use bearings instead of polyurethane or rubber bushings to eliminate side-to-side deflection in the suspension.

2 Fit Arm to Bracket

The upper control arms are fitted to the chassis brackets, secured with the new hardware and are allowed to hang free.

3 Inspect Strut Rod

The lower arms feature an adjustable strut rod, which puts preload on the chassis mounts. One side bolts to the frame in the factory strut location.

4 Locate Frame Mount

Each lower arm is installed to the factory mount in the frame. Note the position of the strut rod.

5 Bolt Arm and Rod Together

The kit comes with new hardware for all of the components. The lower arms and strut rod are bolted together, but not torqued until the weight of the car is on the suspension.

6 Position Axle Assembly

At this stage, you need to get a friend or helper to help move the axle assembly onto a floor jack. With the axle on a floor jack, you can move it into position, then raise or lower it. This allows you to attach the suspension links and ultimately complete the installation of the axle assembly. To facilitate the upper-mount installation, attach the upper suspension links to axle housing first. The upper mounts are tight, so this is the easiest way to get them on.

7 Connect Arm to Chassis Mounts

Next, raise the housing with a floor jack so the lower arm can be connected to the chassis mounts. Slip the bolts through the suspension arm ends and housing mounts.

8 Connect Springs to Housing and Frame

The springs lock onto a stub on the housing and the frame. There is plenty of room for them. Simply position the springs onto the spring nipples on the upper and lower platforms, and raise the housing until the weight of the car is on the springs. Install the shocks onto the upper and lower studs and torque the nuts to the specs provided in the kit.

9 Torque Bolts to Spec

With the rear at ride height (the weight of the car should be on the suspension), torque all of the bolts to spec. Use a quality torque wrench. The factory torque specs are 80 ft-lbs for each control arm bolt, 12 ft-lbs for the upper shock bolt, and 65 ft-lbs for the lower shock mount. Keep in mind that aftermarket kits may have different torque specs and you need to follow the aftermarket manufacturer's instructions.

Project: Updating Inside the Housing

There is more to an axle assembly than just the differential and gears. The housing needs to be inspected, evaluated, and replaced if necessary. Even if you are only changing gear ratios, now is a good time to update the consumables inside the housing. All GM 10- and 12-bolt housings have six sets of bearings and races: two wheel bearings, two for the carrier, and two for the pinion. Although I cover the pinion-and-carrier bearings in Chapter 5, this project starts with the wheel bearings and the races for the pinion bearings. These are installed into the housing itself.

1 Remove Bearings from Center Section

You have two methods for removing the bearing races from the center section. You can use a race driver and a hammer to drive the race from the case, or you can use a large socket that matches the diameter of the race. When using the socket method, you also need to use an extension and a long bar to drive it from the case.

Professional Mechanic Tip

2 Remove Bearings from Center Section *(CONTINUED)*

A bearing race puller has a driving end that fits securely in the race and an extension that threads onto the driving end. Using a bearing puller is the preferred and easier method. Put the socket and extension into the tube and properly align it with the bearing race. Make sure the socket is sitting square on the race.

3 Remove Bearings from Center Section *(CONTINUED)*

Insert the bar into the axle tube after the socket and extension.

4 Remove Bearings from Center Section *(CONTINUED)*

Align the bar inside the socket extension. The bar should be about level with the floor so the socket is squarely engaging the bearing race. Use a hammer to swiftly strike the end of the bar.

The front and then rear pinion races must be removed in this order. Steady the bar and squarely engage the race with the socket. You can use a deadblow hammer (shown) to drive out the race.

Critical Inspection

5 Inspect Bearing Race Bore

With the front race removed, you can see the inner race from the front side of the housing. Closely inspect for any abnormalities or damage. Differentials usually do not experience damage in this area.

6 Inspect Bearing Race

A typical Chevy 10- or 12-bolt rebuild kit has the correct-size bearing races for all bearing surfaces. Inspect them carefully because damage in shipping and defects in manufacturing can occur. Make sure the new race surfaces are clean and true. Installed properly, the axle shafts will perform at their best. Inspect the races before you install them and make sure you use the correct race for the bearing.

7 Install Outer Bearing Race

Properly align the race within the bore so it is square. Place the socket against the edge of the race and make sure it's square as well. Use a hammer to tap against the edge of the race and methodically and carefully drive it into the bore until it is firmly seated in position.

8 Install Outer Bearing Race *(CONTINUED)*

You can feel that the race is fully seated. This is what it looks like when it is seated.

9 Install Inner Bearing Race

Correctly installing the inner race can be difficult because it tends to twist and not stay square in the bore. The case surrounding the bore adds a level of difficulty. When installing the race, use a hammer and socket to slowly and carefully drive it down until it is fully seated in the bore.

Bearings and Races

The race is the machined surface on which the bearing rides, and it's a replaceable component that is usually matched to the bearing. You can reuse the race if the bearings have not failed or been overheated, but you should replace the races when you change the bearings. The pinion bearing races are pressed into the housing. The larger inner bearing is pressed in from the carrier side while the smaller outer pinion bearing is pressed in from the yoke side. Special bearing installation tools are available, but it can be done with a hammer and an appropriate socket.

Wheel bearings are internal bearings and do not have races. Therefore, the bearing is pressed into the axle tube, just inside of the end plate, and the bearings ride on the axle shaft itself. Three types of bearings are offered for axles: standard, repair, and sealed.

Standard Bearings

These typical bearings are found in the axle assembly and are encased in a simple housing as a retainer. They are pressed into the axle tubes and the axle slides through them.

Gear oil must be used to sustain the bearing's lubricity. A seal must be installed after the bearing in order to cap the housing.

Repair Bearings

The bearing surface of the axle could be galled and pitted if your wheel bearings are worn out or damaged, the housing is run without oil, or the bearings have been overheated. The rear axle assembly will howl from the bearing noise and the bearings won't last very long. You have two choices: replace the axle or change to a repair bearing. These bearings use an integral seal that is shorter than a traditional seal, allowing the new bearings to ride farther out on the axle shaft itself, where there is no damage. These bearings are expensive and they don't always work, but it is an option.

Sealed Bearings

This type of bearing seals off the axle without a separate seal. They are used with C-clip eliminator kits for 10- and 12-bolt units. Because of the design, sealed bearings must be pressed onto the axle. They are very good for controlling up-and-down motion because they have no play in

Many home workshops do not have a hydraulic press, but if you do, it allows you to precisely press the races into the housing. Here, the socket and extension are aligned under the press. The next step is to slowly engage the press and watch it press the race into the bore.

them, unlike the standard and repair bearings. However, they are also quite expensive. The sealed bearings for GM 10- and 12-bolts require the above-mentioned eliminator kit.

C-Clip Conversions

C-clip eliminators are required for certain race classes and are often used for high-horsepower applications and off-road vehicles because the wheels on the axle remain with the vehicle. If a C-clip axle breaks, it allows the corresponding wheel to come out from under the car, and that is a very dangerous situation.

A C-clip eliminator replaces the C-clip and provides a much more secure way to retain the axle: The bearings are pressed onto the axles. A plate captures the bearing and also the axle when it is bolted to the housing end. In most cases, installing these eliminators does not require machining the housing, but stock axles do require machine work to ensure that the bearing can be pressed onto the correct area for engagement.

C-clip eliminators are not the only conversion option. You can convert a 10- and 12-bolt axle assembly to a flange-style retainer. But this requires some fabrication work. You need to cut off the existing axle ends

When the underside of the car is tight, using the rear cover may be easier than the front port. Not always though. Some aftermarket housings don't have a side fill port, so the rear cover is the only option. With this car, a hose relocates the bottle above the axle housing.

and weld new ends on the housing. Then you press on Ford 9-inch-style press-on bearing axles; you don't need to install C-clip eliminators for a street application.

Keep in mind, C-clip eliminators are bolted, not welded, to the axle tubes. As a result, the ends can (and often do) flex against the hous-

ing end during extreme use. Nothing will prevent the flexing; not the manufacturer of the ends, their thickness, or the material. It's going to occur. When they flex, the bearings wear out the seals. Sometimes the seals take a few years to wear out, but usually, they wear out in about a year with regular street use.

The Buick and Oldsmobile bolt-in axles are great for performance because there are no C-clips. Unfortunately, most GM 10- and 12-bolts do not have this option.

Bolt-in C-clip eliminators are not really a good option for street cars. The best option for a street car build is welding on new outer wheel bearings and new axles. These 9-inch Ford ends are the best solution if C-clips do not work for your build.

DISASSEMBLY

The disassembly procedure for both Chevy 10- and 12-bolt rear differentials is virtually the same. You do not need to be concerned with getting it out of alignment. As long as you take the proper steps to ensure that the shims go back in the correct location, the entire unit can be disassembled, cleaned, and inspected, with the exception of the pinion gear.

In both units the pinion gear uses a crush sleeve to set the preload on the bearings and removing it requires the installation of a new crush sleeve. So, consider this fair warning.

Although other components do not have to be aligned, you need to keep the inner pinion bearing properly aligned. This bearing is pressed on and removing the bearing instantly changes alignment. Don't remove the bearing unless you are replacing it.

Main Housing

You can work with the axle assembly in the vehicle or on the bench. It really doesn't matter which. There are drawbacks and advantages to both, especially in the set-up phase. Most applications require removing only a few extra bolts to the get the housing out of the vehicle. If you are performing a complete overhaul, taking the housing out of the chassis allows you to clean and paint the housing. However, it's your decision whether or not to unbolt the axle from the chassis. Here are some of the pros and cons you must consider.

If you have the use of a lift, you can more easily remove the entire housing because you aren't on your back under the car to complete the procedure. If you do not have a lift, you need to jack up the car and place it on jackstands. Removal is a bit more difficult. However, removing the housing is often the best way to go because it's much easier to work on the entire housing on a bench or stand rather than still installed in the car.

Once the axle shafts have been removed, you can lift the ring gear and carrier out of the center section. Then the carrier disassembly can commence.

Servicing the Axle Assembly

In the Vehicle

Pros
- Less effort to remove the unit
- Easier to torque the crush sleeve
- Housing can't move around

Cons
- Chassis can be in the way
- Harder to clean and paint
- Heavy parts to lift overhead

Out of the Vehicle

Pros
- Easy to clean and paint
- Easier to set backlash and make adjustments
- Parts removal is simpler

Cons
- Have to remove it from vehicle
- Must secure housing to bench
- Installing crush sleeve is more difficult

Limited-Slip or Open Differential?

You need to determine which differential is in your vehicle. One of the most common questions when looking at an axle assembly is, "Do I have a Posi-Traction (limited-slip) or an open carrier?" There are several ways to answer this question. Most gearheads use the common burnout method: Do a burnout, and if you get two black stripes, you have a working Posi-Traction carrier. This doesn't always work, however. Posi-Traction is a limited-slip design, and over time, the clutches wear out and function essentially as an open carrier.

Another simple test is to jack up the back of the vehicle with the wheels off the ground and the transmission in neutral. Spin the tire and watch which direction the other wheel turns. If it spins in the same direction, it is a Posi. If it spins in the opposite direction, it is an open carrier. Without a load on the clutches, even a worn Posi carrier should function in this manner.

To conclusively determine the type of differential, you can always open the housing and look at the carrier itself. In certain situations, this is the only way to know for sure. Open carriers have four spider gears and a crossbolt. GM Posi units usually have four spider gears, a crossbolt, and a pair of S-shaped springs with a set of four coil springs between two plates in the center of the carrier.

External Inspection

Most axle assembly issues make noise when in operation. Howling, clunking, or banging indicates different issues inside the axle housing. Many signs can tell you that the differential is worn out and may be close to failing. The following is a brief list of signs and their general cause.

Leaks

A small pool of gear oil on the ground by the rear tires or a greasy wheel/tire is a sure sign of a bad axle seal. Often, worn axle bearings cause this condition. You can tell it is gear oil by the color and smell. Gear oil is always dark and it smells horrible. There is nothing else like it.

Don't just replace the seals, you should go ahead and replace the bearings too. If you ignore this sign, the bearing could lock up, which will also lock up that wheel, destroy the tire, break or bend the axle, and possibly wreck the vehicle.

Groaning or Howling

Two things typically cause these sounds: worn bearings or gears out of mesh. Gears usually howl when they have not been set up correctly. In most cases, this is a result of too little or too much backlash as well as not correctly setting the preload on the pinion bearings. Unfortunately, an incorrectly set up differential will damage the ring-and-pinion gears within a hundred miles or so, and correctly resetting the backlash does not eliminate the howling. If the howling appears after many years of use, a worn or damaged bearing is most likely creating the noise.

Six bearings are installed in GM 10- and 12-bolt rear axle assemblies. Two bearings are in the axle ends, two are in the differential carrier bearings, and two are in the pinion bearings.

Knocking or Banging

Worn bearings or improper gear adjustments most often create these noises. Keep in mind that worn-out U-joints in the driveline can also cause clunking sounds; inspect those first to eliminate that possibility. Does the noise happen when shifting, under a load, or when letting off the gas? The following tests can help you localize the issue. It is best to perform these tests on a clear stretch of road without other vehicles around.

Cruising Speed: When driving the vehicle, accelerate up to a speed over 30 mph and maintain that speed. Listen closely for any kind of noises coming from areas of the vehicle other than the axle assembly. Axle assembly noise is usually not heard at a constant speed, unlike engine, suspension, and transmission noises, which can be mistaken for axle assembly noise.

Varying Speed: Many axle issues become evident when you quickly accelerate and decelerate using the throttle. When you do this test, you are loading and unloading the gears and bearings. Clunking or banging is evidence of worn bearings or seriously worn gears.

Coasting: If you hear a howl or whine when the vehicle is coasting, you most likely have a worn-out pinion bearing.

Worn Bearings

With the car parked, jack up the axle assembly and support the vehicle on jack stands. Never get underneath a vehicle supported by just a floor jack. If it fails and you're underneath the car, you can be crushed. Try to lift the wheels to determine if there is any movement in the axle. There should be very little. If the wheel moves up and down, the axle bearings are most likely worn or failing.

Also check the pinion yoke with the same test, after unbolting the U-joint. The pinion bearings could be excessively worn and need replacement if the yoke moves up and down.

Axle Removal

The axle assembly must be rebuilt once you have determined that it is generating noise from worn gears or bearings, leaking a lot of fluid, or has completely failed. If you can completely remove the axle unit from the car, it will be far easier to rebuild on a bench. Different makes and models require different methods to remove

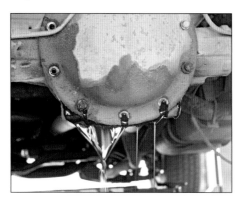

You can work with the housing in or out of the car. It depends on your preference and tools available. The first step is to use a socket and ratchet or a wrench to remove the cover bolts. Use a soft mallet to break the seal or use a pry bar, but be careful not to damage the mounting surface of the center section. Place a drain pan under the center section, and once the cover has been removed, allow the fluid to drain.

Safety

Safety has to be at the top of your list. This means you need to evaluate your physical and mechanical ability to complete each procedure. Do not attempt any procedure that you're uncomfortable performing or you simply cannot do alone. Axle assemblies weigh several hundred pounds and if you drop one you can cause serious injury or death. Please exercise the utmost caution. Get someone else to help when you're moving the axle assembly or large heavy pieces of equipment. You don't want to drop an axle and injure yourself or damage it.

You should wear eye protection when working on axles and when you're handling parts that operate in lubricants; you should also wear nitrile gloves.

the housing. Therefore, I can't cover every removal procedure for specific cars and trucks. But I can explain the most common procedure for removing these axle assemblies.

The first step is to suspend the chassis and let the rear extend freely under the car. Use the properly rated floor jack to jack up the car and place the correct jackstands under the frame rails. Remove the lug nuts and take off the rear wheels. The shocks are fully extended and can be unbolted. Once the shocks have been removed, more of a load is placed on the leaf springs and the axle drops farther.

Brake Lines and Cables

Depending on the length of the brake lines, you may or may not have to remove them before you remove the shocks. You need to ensure the brake lines are correctly routed so they do not contact the exhaust or any moving parts.

It's a good idea to take a photo at this stage of the project so you know how to route the brake lines when you re-install the axle assembly on the vehicle.

You need to remove the parking brake cable. Pull back the boot on the bracket and remove the retaining clip; then the fitting can be removed from the bracket. Use a wrench to remove the flexible brake line fitting on the top of the axle housing.

Driveshaft and Leaf Springs

Next, turn your attention to the driveshaft. First, you need to remove the four bolts that retain the U-joint. These hold the two straps on a GM strap-type driveshaft. Once the bolts have been removed, push the driveshaft forward and the U-joint will separate from the pinion gear yoke.

Remove the leaf springs and then you can move the axle assembly to your workbench for rebuilding.

Corrosion and Rust

The axle assembly and rear suspension on street cars are exposed to corrosion, moisture, and all kinds of debris. As a consequence, they suffer corrosion and rust. If your axle assembly hasn't been removed in years, the retaining bolts and nuts are most likely corroded and it's not going to be an easy job. Here are the steps I use:

Soak the front and rear leaf-spring shackle bolts and nuts with penetrant lube. Use an impact wrench or a 1/2-inch ratchet to remove the front leaf springs nuts.

If the penetrant lube is not sufficient, you may need to use a propane torch or similar device to heat the nuts. Apply heat for at least one minute and if it does not do the trick, try it again.

Extend the floor jack so it is just under the pumpkin (center section) so that when the leaf springs are removed the axle assembly does not hit the floor.

Remove the nut from the front shackle of the leaf spring. Remove the nuts that secure the spring pack and remove the rear shackle bolts.

Once the leaf springs have been removed, you and a helper can roll the axle assembly out from under the car. At this point, you and your assistant can lift the axle assembly onto your workbench.

Fluid

Make sure you have an oil pan or tray underneath the housing to catch the fluid. Use a socket and ratchet to spin off the center section. Use a screwdriver or scraper to gently pry the cover from the housing. A gasket and often silicone sealant hold the cover on, so expect some effort in splitting the cover. Let the fluid drain before moving to the next step.

Inspect the fluid as it drains and then examine it in the catch pan. Chunks of metal are obvious signs of a major gear or component failure. If the fluid is shimmering with silver streaks or flecks, you know you have metal wear on the inside of the unit. If you see this, do not ignore it, you need to replace all the bearings and races inside your housing.

When differential fluid is new, it is clear. Many miles of use causes the fluid's color to gradually change as it absorbs heat and provides lubrication. Water and dirt contaminate the fluid and it quickly turns dark. At the end of its life cycle, the fluid is very dark. Moreover, any old oil residue from the old oil changes the color of new oil in short order. The primary things to look for are signs of metal wear and overheated oil, which smells burned, but even that can be tricky with gear oil.

Gear Mesh

You can check the mesh between the gears by holding the carrier with one hand and rotating the pinion yoke. It should move a little, but it should not be loose. If you want to determine the exact amount, mount a dial indicator and take the measurement. This is an unnecessary step if you are rebuilding the unit.

Pinion Yoke Removal

A large nut secures the pinion gear to the pinion yoke. Using an impact wrench is the easiest way to remove the nut. If you don't have air tools, you can use a breaker bar and socket to remove it by hand. First, you need to lock the axles from spinning.

This can be done with a helper or by setting a box-end wrench on one lug of an axle and letting it rotate until it locks against the workbench or the shop floor. Once you break the tension on the pinion nut, you should be able to remove it easily.

It is much easier to work on an axle assembly on jack stands, rather than installed in the car. If you're not performing a complete rebuild, it often makes sense to leave it installed in the car. On the other hand, if you are performing a complete rebuild, it makes much more sense to remove it from the vehicle. In this case, the 12-bolt has been removed from the chassis, and it's being completely rebuilt.

1 Remove Pinion Nut

A fair amount of torque is required for removing the pinion nut. If the axles have been removed, it's difficult to prevent the pinion from moving when trying to remove the nut because the axles provide resistance. However, the axles can be held tight so that the pinion doesn't spin. Impact tools do the job. Note the thick washer behind the pinion yoke nut.

2 Remove Yoke

A few blows with a soft hammer usually gets the yoke free from the splines. Tap on one side and then the other so it slides off the spline. Make sure to use a soft hammer because you don't want to damage the yoke. Once the axle has been rebuilt, the yoke can be reinstalled if it is not damaged.

3 Remove Pinion Seal

Special Tool

The pinion seal is positioned at the end of the tail section. A seal removal tool quickly and safely extracts the seal from the end of the housing. Or you can use a medium-size cold chisel to remove the seal. Run the tool around the lip of the seal to start the process. Tap on one side of the seal, then switch to the other side so it comes off evenly and does not become cocked in the housing end.

Axle Shaft Removal

Most GM 10- and 12-bolt axle assemblies have C-clips retaining the axles, but some Buick, Oldsmobile, and Pontiac 10-bolt housings have bolt-in axles. Remove the disc brakes or drum brakes before you proceed. You need to remove the drum brake cover and then remove the brackets that retain the brake shoes. At this step, you should be able to determine the style of ring gear carrier in the axle: open, limited-slip, or locker.

Each of them can be removed using the following procedures.

On the carrier, a center pin runs through two of the four spider gears. A small bolt holds one end of this pin onto the carrier. This bolt is just to the side of the center of the carrier; remove it using a socket and a wrench. The end of the bolt has a long pin. With the bolt out, the center drift pin should slide out easily from the carrier. You may need to rotate the carrier to get the pin clear of the case. Now, the axles can be pushed into the housing from the outside.

If the assembly has C-clip axles, the clips are on the end of the axles. Pull them off and the axles will slide out of the carrier and can be removed from the housing.

If the axles are bolted in, there are no clips and you will not be able to push the axles into the housing. In this case, follow this procedure: Four nuts on the end of the axle tubes hold the drum brake backing plates to the housing and bolt-in axles. They also secure the axle retainers. Remove these nuts with a wrench or socket, and the axle and backing plates will separate from the housing.

You may want to remove the brake backing plates on bolt-in and C-clip housings if you plan to paint the case.

1 Remove Center Pin

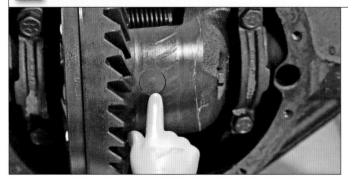

In the process of removing the pinion yoke, you need to remove the center pin. The center pin is in the middle of the carrier; it holds the yoke to the pinion gear.

2 Remove Pin Bolt

The pin bolt retains the center pin; to remove the center pin you need to remove the bolt.

3 Remove Pin Bolt (CONTINUED)

Use a ratchet, extension, and a 1/2-inch socket to turn out the pin bolt. An extension is required in order to clear the carrier bearing cap.

4 Drive Down Center Pin

Use a large flat punch and a hammer to drive out the pin. Be patient and take your time when tapping it out. Sometimes it doesn't require much effort so don't use heavy blows; other times the center pin slides right out. If the pin is stuck or stubborn, use a soft brass punch to get it moving. But don't drive it all the way out just yet.

5 Move Carrier into Position

Roll back or rotate the carrier so the other side of the pin is exposed. Use pliers to pull it out. Try not to damage the pin's surface; you may be able to reuse it.

6 Properly Store Parts

Be sure to properly organize and store your parts. Have a box or tub handy to store all the hardware. At this stage, do not dispose of any parts; keep all of them. Some will be replaced, and some will be reused.

Carrier Removal

A pair of main caps fastens the carrier inside case, and these caps are designated for a particular position. An arrow on the main caps usually points towards the axle tubes, indicating the direction that the cap should face. Use a grease pencil, paint marker, or hammer stamp to mark both the cap and the housing for each cap so the caps are installed in the same place and correctly oriented. Remove the two bolts per cap and set them aside. The caps require some effort to remove them from the case because of the tight fit. A plastic mallet or hammer can be used to tap them out; alternatively, a screwdriver or pry tool can be used to ease them out. You want to work them from the top and bottom. Don't just pry on one end because they sit in a deep relief and are easily cracked.

With the caps out, the carrier can be removed. There are shims on either side of the carrier bearing races. Most stock units use cast shims, but if the housing has been rebuilt before, there may be multiple shims. The stock rings are very fragile, and if they fall, they may shatter. Having a second set of hands to help catch them is very handy here. The carrier fits tight to the housing; you will need the pry tool to slowly wedge the carrier out of the housing. Label the shims to match the side they came from; if you get them backward, the alignment will never be right.

1 Remove Axle Shafts

To remove the axles, the C-clips have to come out. The axle assembly should be positioned on jack stands or a bench. You can use your hands or a block of wood to push the axle shaft toward the center section. Push the axles in as far as they will go.

2 Remove Axle Shafts (CONTINUED)

The axle shaft end extends into the center of the carrier and gives you the room needed to remove it. This C-clip (arrow) is just below the axle end flange.

3 Remove Axle Shafts (CONTINUED)

Special Tool

Several methods can be used to extract the C-clip from the carrier housing. You can use a pick, screwdriver, or wire hook. A magnet tool is the best method of removing the C-Clip.

4 Remove Axle Shafts (CONTINUED)

Now you can slide the axle shafts out of the axle tubes. Grab hold of the hubs and pull the shafts out. If the bearings are damaged or seized, the axles may be difficult to remove. With enough effort you should be able to pull them out of the housing.

5 Identify and Mark Axle Shafts

Axle shafts are the same length from side to side, but you should reinstall one in the same axle tube it was originally removed from, especially if you are not replacing bearings. Take this opportunity to mark each side.

6 Find Main Bearing Caps

A pair of main caps holds the carrier in place. These are side- and top-bottom specific.

7 Mark Main Bearing Caps

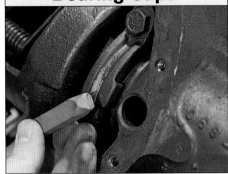

Use a number or letter stamp to mark the cap and its respective side. You can use a paint marker too.

Professional Mechanic Tip **PRO TIP**

8 Remove Main Bearing Caps

PRO TIP You can use a socket and a breaker bar to remove the main bearing caps. But I recommend using an impact gun to loosen the caps. Then you can remove them by hand.

9 Remove Carrier and Ring Gear

With the main bearing caps removed, you can see the bearing race (top arrow) and a cast-iron shim (bottom arrow).

10 Remove Carrier and Ring Gear
(CONTINUED)

Pull straight back on the carrier to slide it out. A significant amount of force is required to get it moving, but once it does, the carrier slides right out.

11 Remove Carrier Shims

Carefully remove, tag, and store the shims. If these fall to the garage floor, they will break. Use a Sharpie and some tape to mark each shim and designate its installation side.

Pinion Removal

At this point, the pinion gear is exposed. If you are not changing gear ratios or the pinion bearings, there is no need to go any further. However, when you disassemble the axle, you might as well replace it all.

Use a soft-blow hammer or mallet to tap the pinion out of the case from the front side; you need to hit the yoke side of the gear to remove the pinion. Remove the small-diameter bearing on the front side behind the seal along with a flat washer. Keep the washer, as it will be reused. You can remove the seal before or after the gear; it really doesn't matter.

The second pinion bearing is a large bearing pressed onto the gear, and it can only be removed with a press. There should also be a crush sleeve on the gear shaft.

Several races should be replaced because after extreme use or high mileage they are most often worn. Use a brass driver or a race driver/removal tool kit to tap each race out of the case. The races on the axle tubes for the axle bearings are difficult to remove because you need a long bar to reach them from the inside.

Here's a handy tip to drive out the race: Place a large socket that matches the diameter of the bearing race inside the axle tube. Guide a piece of heavy tubing or bar through the opposite end of the axle tube until the socket rests up against the bearing race. Use a hammer to hit the bar and drive out the race. Repeat for the other side.

1 Remove Pinion Gear

With the carrier and related parts removed from the center section you have room to drive the pinion gear out of the housing. Use a soft hammer to tap on the threaded end of the pinion gear and drive it into the axle housing. If the axle assembly has not been damaged, the pinion should come out with a few taps.

Important!

2 Remove Pinion Gear
(CONTINUED)

If the pinion gear is stubborn and binds up, use a ballpeen hammer to drive it out. But you must protect the gear threads if you are going to reuse the pinion. If that is the case, thread the pinion nut back onto the pinion and use a bigger hammer. The pinion nut is always replaced so you don't need to worry about damaging it.

3 Remove Pinion Gear (CONTINUED)

If the pinion gear still does not slide out of the housing, you can put the pinion and housing in a press. You have to be careful here because too much pressure could break the housing. If you put it in a press and it doesn't move with a couple tons of force, you need to stop. Another method is to apply heat to get the pinion gear to move.

4 Remove Pinion Gear (CONTINUED)

This 12-bolt passenger car housing had been run low on gear oil, so it overheated and the front pinion bearing seized onto the pinion shaft. I used an oxyacetylene torch to heat up the pinion gear but I am careful not to apply too much heat in any one area.

5 Remove Pinion Gear *(CONTINUED)*

This is a severe case and I hope you don't have to take such extreme measures. Running this axle without fluid created some difficult problems in disassembly. In the end, I used a torch to cut the bearing and free the pinion.

Critical Inspection

6 Inspect Pinion Gear

Lack of lubrication in an axle assembly typically causes bad things to happen such as catastrophic failure. You can see the scarring on the pinion. With this kind of scoring, it cannot be reused. I will need a new pinion and ring when I reassemble this axle.

Cleaning the Housing

I usually pressure wash the entire housing and axle tubes. If you don't have a pressure washer, you could take them to a self-serve, manual car wash. Or you can apply a lot of degreaser, such as brake cleaner, and use a lot of rags to strip the grease, oil, and other gunk out of the housing. You need to ensure that the entire axle assembly is thoroughly cleaned so the axle components don't fail prematurely or underperform because of contaminants in the bearings, components, and oil. Cleanliness is very important for bearing health.

Do not leave the axle exposed to elements. Once you have cleaned it, coat the surfaces with WD-40 to prevent oxidation or rust. If you are looking for a deep clean on your housing, especially if you plan on painting the unit, you might want to look into one of the following cleaning methods.

Although some enthusiasts own media blasting equipment, many do not own the other cleaning equipment. You may need to call the shops in your area to see if they have suitable cleaning equipment for your project.

Blasting

Media blasting is an excellent way to clean the housing and can be done at home with a portable unit or you can find a local blaster to do the job for you. To clean the case, you can use several types of media: walnut shells, baking soda, crushed glass. Remember that you need to protect several precision finishes in your housing, so I recommend that you avoid using sand.

Walnut shells and baking soda are the best blast media for a housing because they don't damage any of the precision surfaces. In addition, walnut shells are not highly abrasive and therefore don't generate much heat (no warping), and are environmentally friendly.

If you use baking soda, be sure to neutralize the soda residue with a vinegar and water mixture before painting.

However neither walnut shells nor baking soda can touch rust. If the housing is just a little rusty, you can clean it by hand, or you can use crushed glass. Crushed glass does not release free silica so it's safe for the environment. And it's less likely to damage precision surfaces as long as you have some experience.

Hot Tanking

A true hot tank uses an acid/water bath to strip away grease, grime, rust scale, and almost anything else on the surface of an axle assembly. Many shops no longer use this method because the acid is a hazardous substance and EPA permits are required.

If you can find a working hot tank, have your axle assembly cleaned in it because they do a better job than any other method. Just make sure you neutralize the acid before painting.

Wash Tanking

A wash tank is an environmentally safe equivalent to the hot tank. These are essentially large dishwasher-type units that use near-boiling water and detergent to clean the parts. If you can find one large enough to fit an axle assembly, it can do the job.

Brake Conversions for GM 10- and 12-Bolt Axles

You can select and install a variety of OEM and aftermarket brake systems for GM 10- and 12-bolt rear assemblies. Many of these housings that were built from the 1960s to the 1980s were fitted with drum brakes from the factory. Beginning in the early 1990s, rear disc brakes were more commonly installed on GM 10-bolt rears, and, eventually, just about all the Chevy 10-bolt axles have discs from the factory. Finding a factory disc-brake 10-bolt is pretty easy if you are working with an F-Body (Camaro/Firebird), but if you have an original GM 12-bolt, you need to look at the aftermarket.

Front Brake Choices

Factory drum brakes have the lowest level of brake performance, but it may be adequate for street cruising with restored cars or mild resto-mods. If you are building a high-performance car, there is no substitute for disc brakes. Defining your performance requirements and budget will help you determine the best system for your vehicle.

You could pull a newer factory GM disc brake system from a salvage yard car; it's a definite improvement over the factory drum brakes. However, it's a marginal improvement because you are still dealing with factory braking performance. As you probably already know, an aftermarket brake system from a popular manufacturer, such as Baer or Wilwood, provides the best performance for the money. With everything from single-piston calipers and 11-inch rotors all the way up to massive six-piston units with 14-inch discs, you can find a brake set for every application.

Rear Brake Selection Factors

Choosing the rear brakes depends on several factors: front brakes, wheel size, and intended use. If you drag race your car with little street time, lightweight rear discs are a better choice than six-piston calipers.

Front Brakes

This is the most important aspect for safety and control. You don't want big rear brakes and small front brakes. When a car slows down, it transfers vehicle weight from the rear to the front of the car. Consequently, the front brakes perform most of the work and therefore most vehicles carry front brake rotors that are larger than rear brake rotors.

Under braking, the rear carries less weight and if the rear brakes are too large, they can lock up before the front. The car goes into a slide and the driver loses control of the car. This is a dangerous situation and should be avoided.

The rear brakes should always be at least the same size as the fronts, but most builders use slightly smaller brakes in the rear. If you just have to have large rear brakes, you need to install a proportioning valve and set the rear brake pressure quite low.

Wheel Size

The size of the wheels you are running plays a large role in how big the rear brakes can be. If you have stock 15-inch steel wheels from just about any 1970s or earlier car, you might not even be able to fit 11-inch disc brakes, depending on the inner wheel lip, especially on trucks. Check your wheels before you order parts and make sure your brakes will fit. The 13-inch brakes generally use 17- to 18-inch wheels or larger.

Intended Use

Street cars and road race vehicles have different braking demands than drag cars. Many applications cross over between the intended uses, but there are drag-race-only rear brakes that should not be used on street cars. Just be aware of the intended use when you are looking for brakes.

Rear Disc Brake Components

Rear disc brake systems have three main components: calipers, pads, and rotors. All of these components (plus the emergency brake) work together and are not generally chosen separately. Each has its own selection guidelines.

Calipers

A variety of calipers are available from single-piston to six-piston for most aftermarket brakes. In essence, the disc brake caliper is a hydraulic clamp that pushes one pad against another with the spinning rotor in between.

More efficient and effective than drum brakes, the disc brake has evolved through the years. There is nothing "wrong" with a single-piston caliper, but six smaller pistons spread the load more evenly, providing better stopping power and better wear characteristics so the pads last longer.

Brake Conversions for GM 10- and 12-Bolt Axles CONTINUED

Caliper material is a big factor in brake performance. Cast-iron frames hold heat longer, so the pads and rotors stay hotter, decreasing their effectiveness. Aluminum frames dissipate heat much faster and are lighter weight, but they also cost more.

Pads

The brake pads and shoes for drums are the main wearable components of the braking system. Four common types of pads/shoes are available: semi metallic, non-asbestos organic (NAO), low-metallic NAO, and ceramic. NAO and low-metallic NAO versions are commonly found at parts stores, but ceramic pads are becoming more readily available.

NAO pads are softer and produce less noise than semi-metallics, but they wear fast and make a lot of dust.

Low-metallic pads wear better than NAO pads, but still make dust and tend to run noisier.

Ceramic pads are the best, using ceramic fibers, non-ferrous fillers, and small amounts of metal. They are much quieter and produce less dust and they don't wear down the rotors nearly as fast. However, ceramic pads are much more expensive at about twice the price of an NAO pad. But they do last longer and are more efficient, so take that into consideration.

Rotors

The other wearable component in the braking system is the rotor/drum. Like a flywheel, the rotor/drum surface is where the action is, and they do wear down. A typical stock rotor may feature a gas port or slot. As the pads heat up in the rotor, they produce gases. These gases need to be released or they can inhibit braking efficiency.

High-performance rotors typically use a combination of slots and cross-drilled holes to port the gases. You need to follow the manufacturer's installation instructions and be sure the slots are facing the correct direction; otherwise, brake performance will be degraded. In addition, the orientation of the discs varies from manufacturer to manufacturer. Closely inspect cross-drilled rotors because these can crack at the holes due to heating and cooling cycles and stress risers in the drilled area.

Chamfered holes remove the stress risers and help to eliminate the potential for stress cracks. Most high-end rotors now feature chamfered or relieved cross drilling.

Although solid rotors are still available, you should avoid them for high-performance applications because the solid rotors do not dissipate heat as well as slotted, grooved, or cross-drilled rotors. The rotor should be vented around the perimeter to increase cooling. Solid rotors may warp under heavy use.

Wheel size also needs to be considered when buying brakes. Increasing the size of the rotors may make using stock wheels impossible. For example, a 13-inch rotor doesn't fit in a stock 14- or 15-inch wheel and typically requires a 17-inch or larger wheel.

Line Locks

Many cars do not have a line lock and many do not require one. It's commonly used for drag racing, burnouts, and security. The line lock, or "roll control," is an electric valve that holds pressure on one half of the brake lines. This device typically locks the front brakes for rear-wheel-drive cars when the brake pedal is released.

In burnouts and drag racing, the line lock holds the car in place while the driver either spins the tires or loads the engine for a launch. Hit the button, and the brakes are instantly released, letting the car launch hard for more consistent and faster starts.

The other use is for security. If the brakes are locked, it makes it really difficult for a thief to take the car. This is a very useful trick as a secondary anti-theft device.

Master Cylinder

You need to recognize the difference in hydraulic pressure required to operate drum brakes versus disc brakes and the master cylinder's role for supplying pressure to these different setups.

Disc brake calipers require much less hydraulic pressure than drum brake wheel cylinders to properly operate. When you replace rear drum brakes with disc brakes, the master cylinder may not have capacity to provide the correct hydraulic pressure so that they operate properly. You need to be sure to check it more often that you might with drum brakes because drums tend to drain a master cylinder bowl faster.

Also, some drum brake master cylinders have built-in residual valves that hold pressure on the rear line to keep the wheel cylinder from backing off all the way. Typically, drums use a 10-pound valve while disc brake calipers only need a residual valve when the master cylinder is mounted under the floor of the of the car. In this case, a 2-pound valve is used. ∎

Pressure Washing

A pressure washer is one way to clean an axle assembly at home, and you won't anger a car wash owner by leaving a large spot of grease on the car wash floor. Soak the housing with a degreaser (even oven cleaner works quite well), let it sit for the specified amount of time, and then spray away.

If the axle assembly has never been rebuilt, it's often very dirty; some of these housings are 40 years old. If that's the case, the axle is likely to have loads of caked-on grime. You should expect that the axle is going to shed a lot of grease and grime so plan accordingly. It usually takes two to three washings to get it all clean.

Project: 12-Bolt Brake Conversion for a 1967 Chevy Truck

GM 12-bolt axle assemblies use C-clips to hold the axle shafts in the axle tubes. The C-shaped steel clip slides into a groove around the axle about 1/4 inch from the end. The clip pushes against the spider gear or limited-slip plate while a steel bar (held in place with a small pin bolt) keeps the axles from pushing toward the middle of the carrier.

Some GM 10-bolt housings and Ford 9-inch housing use bolt-in axles. Pressed-on bearings and a plate on the outer tubes retains the axles, and the backing plates bolt to this.

Once the axles are out and the backing plates are off, the rest is a simple bolt-in process. A kit from Classic Performance Parts was installed on my 1967 shop truck, and it uses Cadillac calipers and replacement parts for the brakes. The brackets are well designed and easy to install. The edges are quite sharp, so you should wear gloves when handling them. The Cadillac calipers feature integrated parking brakes, so there is a secondary parking brake similar to some other kits.

This kit also included new parking brake cables that connect to the factory cable under the frame, which is a nice touch.

One note about a rear disc brake swap: You have to replace the axles if you have six-lug axles and want to change to five-lugs. Many axle manufacturers offer these conversions from

This 1967 Chevy truck has a 12-bolt truck rear differential and drum brakes, and I want far better performance from the rear brakes than drum brakes can deliver. In addition, the 12-bolt has plenty of miles on it so it needs a rebuild.

basic stock axles to high-performance units. The 12-bolt GM housing is quite stout, and many performance options are offered.

If you want to swap bolt patterns, now is the time. I chose to keep the six-bolt pattern. The previously installed front discs conversion retained the six-bolt pattern as well.

The entire process only took a few hours and the results were impressive, the truck stops better than before with just the front discs, and I retained the six-lug bolt pattern.

1 Remove Wheels

Remove all the lug nuts and take off the wheels. This is a six-lug-axle truck, and this lug nut set from Classic Performance Parts (CPP) retains the wheels.

2 Remove Brake Drum Cover

Many vehicles have old, rusty drums that can be difficult to remove. A subtle tap with a hammer knocks the brake shoes loose from the brake drum.

3 Remove C-Clips

Use a ratchet and socket to remove all the bolts retaining the differential cover. Rotate the carrier into the proper position and remove the center pin. If the pin sticks, you can use a hammer and brass punch to drive out the center pin. Push the axles in to the center and pull out the C-clips. Then pull out the axles.

4 Remove Drum Backing Plates

These bolts tend to be rusty so you may need to use penetrant lube and/or heat. Use a wrench or socket and ratchet to remove the four bolts retaining the plates to the axle tube ends. The brake shoe assemblies lift off once all the retaining bolts have been removed so there's no need to disassemble the mechanisms.

5 Remove Emergency Brake Cables

To fully remove the backing plates, the emergency brake cables must be removed as well. Use Vise-Grips to stretch the cable; then unhook the ball end from the bracket on the brake shoe. If you are replacing the brakes (as I am here), disconnect the parking brake cables at the trailing arms as they will be replaced.

6 Install Emergency Brake Cable Links

The Classic Performance Parts emergency brake kit comes with new cables to link to the original cable. These attach to the original cable clips just as the originals did. The cable is not under tension because it is not connected to the caliper. Therefore you can simply push the ball through the clip and pull it into place in the narrow slot.

7 Install Calipers on Axle Ends

Some brackets may require modification to fit a particular vehicle. In this case, the brackets fit the Chevy 12-bolt axle housing and no additional modifications were necessary.

8 Bolt Brackets to Axle Ends

The brackets bolt to the backside of the axle ends as did the original drum brake backing plates. Make sure the orientation matches that in the instructions. Properly align the bracket under the axle ends and torque down the bolts with a socket and ratchet. The bracket ends face forward toward the front of the car so you can mount the caliper to it.

9 Install Axle Shafts

The axle shafts are fed through the axle tubes and extend into the center of the differential. Hand install the C-Clip over each axle shaft end and then use a socket and ratchet to install the differential center pin.

10 Install Brake Rotors

Line up the lugs with the holes in the rotor and slide each rotor over the axle pads. You can secure the rotor to the axle with a lug nut so it doesn't slide off.

This is a mechanically actuated Cadillac rear caliper with built-in emergency brakes. This eliminates the need for a second caliper.

11 Mount Calipers to Brackets

Insert both brake pads into the caliper. Slide the caliper over the rotor, and then bolt it to the new brackets using the supplied hardware. Most calipers are torqued to between 20 and 30 ft-lbs but you must follow the torque specs included with the instructions.

12 Install Cable Locks

The emergency-brake cable locks into the lever through the return spring. Be sure that the cable end is secure in the tab. You can add a zip-tie to keep it in place before the emergency brake is set.

13 Bleed Brake System

Don't forget to bleed the brake system! You can use a pressure or vacuum bleeder or the two-man system where one person pumps and holds pressure on the pedal while the second person opens the bleeder screw releasing air and fluid. Start at the farthest corner from the master cylinder and move toward the closest corner. Work each caliper until there is no more air coming out of the brakes.

Brake Upgrade for 1971 Buick Gran Sport

A set of 17-inch Centerline wheels were already on this car, so I had the room in the wheels to go with a larger-than-stock brake kit. Being on a budget, I had to search a little. Sure, I could spend $8,000 on six-piston calipers and rotors to go with them, but that is overkill. Finally, I found that the SSBC 13-inch Tri-Power disc brake kit along with their 11-inch single-piston rear disc conversion kit came in at right around $3,500. The kit comes with everything needed to install them, including a new power booster and master cylinder.

The main consideration for this Buick install was the bolt-in axles. If you don't realize that the axles are bolt-in for the Buick rears, you end up wasting a lot of time taking the rear cover off when it isn't necessary. Other than that, the install is fairly straightforward.

1 Unbolt Axles

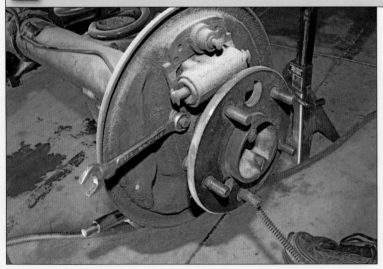

The Buick GS has bolt-in axles, so the rear cover can stay on. Unbolt the axles after the brakes are disassembled. The axles are retained by the same four bolts that hold the backing plates to the axle housing ends.

SSBC brake kits use powder-coated steel brackets that look great and fit well.

2 Install Caliper Brackets on Axle Ends

Because the bolt-in axles seal through the outer bearing, the kit uses a more complex bracket with spacers to properly position the calipers over the rotors. A shim installs between the axle plate and bearing as well.

3 Install Axle Shafts

Reinstall the axle into the housing and torque to 40 lbs. The new hardware is included in the kit. Don't forget to install the gasket. Use a back-up wrench and tighten the bolts in the common star torquing pattern.

4 Install Brake Rotor

Slide the 12-inch rotor onto the axle and install the caliper. The brake pads can slide in with one bolt in the caliper.

Brake Upgrade for 1971 Buick Gran Sport *CONTINUED*

5 Install Proportioning Valve

Retrofit disc brake kits often require a proportioning valve such as this. It has a gauge so you can see the actual pressure. Without this valve, the rear brakes can lock up before the fronts, causing a dangerous loss of control.

Testing the New Brakes

After I installed the brake kit, I bled the system using DOT 5 silicone-based fluid for the all-new system. Then I set out to do some testing.

Proportioning Valve

The SSBC kit comes with an adjustable proportioning valve to adjust the brake bias from front to rear. This is not an essential device, and it isn't needed for most street cars. Therefore, it isn't installed unless you need it for a particular application.

When testing any brake system, you must be sure that the rear brakes do not lock up before the front brakes. If that does happen, you have too much hydraulic pressure going to the rear brakes. After a few hard-braking tests that end up with the back end of the car pitching sideways, I knew I needed the proportioning valve.

This valve must be installed after the distribution block; otherwise the system may not work correctly. I placed the proportioning valve above the axle assembly where the hard line meets the flexible line to the rear brakes. This was a convenient location and lets me see the handy pressure gauge that came with the kit.

Rear brakes need between 600 and 1,200 psi to operate properly, depending on the brake system, front-to-rear weight ratio, and tire width. The minimum brake pressure is 600 psi so it must never fall below this under any circumstance. I set the rear discs to run in the 800 to 900 psi range because it is a nose-heavy convertible with 9-inch-wide tires. The gauge on the valve makes it easy to see current brake pressure, so you don't have to do as much trial-and-error testing.

Braking Computer

With the brakes finally dialed in, I set up the Vericom VC3000 braking computer in the car and did a series of tests. During the test, I did three runs each, 0–30–0 and 0–60–0. It was the same number of tests I did before the brakes were swapped. The results were impressive. In the 30–0 test, the OEM disc brakes stopped the 3,800-pound Buick in 2.96 seconds and it required 70.13 feet. These numbers were determined by averaging the three runs. The SSBC brakes took only 1.92 seconds and 47.56 feet to bring the Buick to a stop. That is a difference of 22.57 feet and 1.4 seconds.

In the 60–0 tests, the results were equally impressive. The stock system required 5.96 seconds and 208.21 feet, which felt like an eternity, but the SSBC system only needed 3.67 seconds and 144.8 feet, a difference of 63.41 feet and 2.29 seconds. The 63-foot difference was substantial, and it could easily mean the difference between avoiding an accident and being involved in one. ∎

ASSEMBLY

A fairly simple mechanical device is used in many different applications to transfer rotational forces. In a car, the differential maintains drivability in varying conditions. It alters how the vehicle negotiates turns as opposed to having both rear wheels spinning at the same speed; the inside wheel is allowed to rotate at a slower speed than the outside wheel. Several types of differentials are used in automotive applications. Each has

its own benefits and drawbacks. For example, an open-type differential is suitable for common highway use, but on the drag strip or rock crawling it wastes power and zaps momentum. Figuring out what kind of differential you need for your application is a key aspect of your build.

The available differentials on the market are open, limited-slip, locking, and spool. The axles are tied together permanently with the

spool, so technically, it is not a differential at all because there is no differentiating rotation between the axles. However, spools are used for certain applications.

Open Differentials

Open differentials comprise the following components. The housing (or case) carries all of the gears. Side gears are the gears that are connected to the axles. Pinion or spider gears ride on the side gears, allowing the differential rotational action. The center (or cross) pin performs several functions as it runs through the pinion gears. This is the shaft on which the pinion gears spin. In addition, the cross pin keeps the axles from sliding inward, locking them in place. Differential side bearings allow the carrier to spin in the case. The ring gear is part of the main gear set, and it bolts to the carrier.

When the vehicle is traveling straight, both tires are spinning at the same rate. This means that the force on the differential side gears is the same. When the differential is operating in this manner, the pinion gears do not spin, so the power is transferred equally to both wheels.

You can see the limited-slip clutch pack through the window of the carrier. The clutch pack senses when a wheel is spinning and directs the torque to the wheel that has traction.

When the vehicle enters a corner, the loads begin to vary and the outside tire travels farther than the inside tire. At this point, the differential pinion or spider gears spin to allow smooth turning without any tire noise or chirping. For most vehicles, this is just fine and rarely presents a problem, until you find yourself on a slippery surface such as snow, ice, or mud. When an open differential senses low traction, it simply allows the slipping tire to spin; if the other tire has good grip, it won't matter, as the mechanical gearing has no kind of locking feature.

In performance applications, the open differential does not supply enough traction. Accelerating quickly overloads the traction capabilities of the tires, resulting in spinning one tire down the road, earning the open carrier names such as "one-tire fryer" or "peg-leg."

Some folks try to solve this condition by welding the spider gears to the side gears. This essentially turns an open carrier into a fully locked carrier. But this is not the right solution. You should avoid doing this because a street car needs the rear tires to spin at different rates in turns, otherwise cornering is severely compromised. Welded spider gears are not very safe. If the welds brake, it could lead to a catastrophic failure of the complete axle assembly, causing a serious accident.

Another way to alter the open carrier case is by using a drop-in or "lunchbox" locker. This replaces the spider gears completely. The drop-in unit locks the axles together when in a straight line and then unlocks through turns with a ratcheting action. These will be discussed further in Chapter 5.

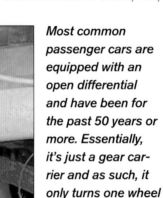

Most common passenger cars are equipped with an open differential and have been for the past 50 years or more. Essentially, it's just a gear carrier and as such, it only turns one wheel at a time under load. These are installed on common passenger cars and are suitable for typical street driving. However, they are not suitable for high-performance cars. These cars need a limited-slip differential for transferring an enormous amount of torque and maximizing traction.

If you see a set of black stripes on the ground, the vehicle almost certainly is equipped with a limited slip, a locker, or a spool. An open differential cannot transfer the torque evenly to both wheels.

The open carrier uses a set of side gears with corresponding spider gears. It has no clutch pack or locking mechanism, and therefore has no device to prevent the over-application of torque to either wheel.

Limited-Slip Differentials

Limited-slip differentials (LSDs) perform as the label implies. This type of differential allows either side to slip a limited amount before locking the axles together so that they spin at the same rate. A limited slip is installed in most muscle cars and high-performance

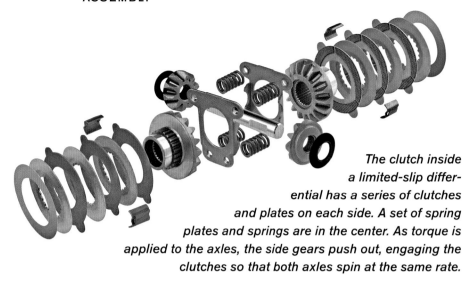

A limited-slip differential uses clutches, cones, or gears to lock the two axles together while allowing them to spin at different rates when needed, such as during cornering. This is a clutch-type Eaton Posi-Traction unit. (Photo Courtesy Eaton)

The clutch inside a limited-slip differential has a series of clutches and plates on each side. A set of spring plates and springs are in the center. As torque is applied to the axles, the side gears push out, engaging the clutches so that both axles spin at the same rate.

vehicles because this affordable differential effectively transmits torque to the ground. Best known by the GM names Posi-Traction (Chevy), Positive Traction (Buick), Anti Spin (Cadillac and Oldsmobile), and Saf-T-Track (Pontiac), the LSD has been used by just about every manufacturer at some point. This style of differential is designed to transfer power from "the wheel that slips to the wheel that grips," or so the commercials used to say. To do this, the limited-slip uses either gears or friction clutches and cones to allow the axles to spin at different rates. Both styles have their advantages and drawbacks, depending on how the vehicle is to be used.

Two types of LSDs are used in automotive applications: clutch (or cone) and gear-driven. These designs have been around for more than 50 years. Over the decades, better manufacturing processes and advanced materials have increased strength and durability, but the principles of operation remain essentially unchanged. GM factory Posi-Traction units found in 10- and 12-bolt axle assemblies were all clutch-type units. The clutches and springs wear out over time but they are rebuildable. Gear-driven LSDs have been used in factory applications, but not in the 10- and 12-bolt housings. They are available in the aftermarket for these housings however, and have become increasingly popular because they are stronger and do not wear out as the clutch/cone units do.

Gear-Driven LSDs

Gear-driven LSDs are becoming much more popular. Eaton's Truetrac was the first LSD to use helical gears over clutches, thus eliminating the wearable clutches and further reducing the chattering clutch noise.

A gear drive is technically not a limited slip; rather, gears are actually torque multipliers instead of controlling slip through a clutch/cone system. As one wheel loses traction, the gears spin and transfer power to the wheel that is gripping. Once a tire has completely lost traction, the LSD operates as if it is an open differential, except that the slipping tire receives no torque. The benefit of the geared LSD is that the application of torque is moderated by engine speed and tire slippage, which makes it easier to get the vehicle out of stuck situations.

The geared LSD is well suited for drag racing, drifting, and road racing. Not all geared LSD units are created equal. Icy conditions can cause traction problems for street cars equipped with geared LSDs because these differentials free wheel in no-traction situations, and this can result in a loss of control. In this situation, applying light pressure to the brakes or using the emergency brake puts enough load on the axle to send torque through a particular wheel. This can be considered a drawback of the gear drive, but not all geared limited slips have this issue.

Some units feature a bias plate that maintains a supply of torque to both wheels. The Truetrac, a helical-gear-type limited-slip, provides smooth power delivery in poor traction situations and makes an excellent choice for hauling heavy payloads and trailering. It is also an excellent front axle application choice for a vehicle that is both a daily driver and a regular off-roader. The biggest benefits are the low-maintenance design as well as smooth and quiet operation. When the clutch-type differential chatters and alters the ability to steer the car, such as with a 2-way-clutch LSD, the gear-drive differential does not.

Geared limited-slip units, such as this Truetrac from Eaton, eliminate the maintenance and strength issues of a clutch-type limited-slip differential. These are good for 650 hp on street tires or 500 hp on slicks. (Photo Courtesy Eaton)

The Wavetrac is Moser's version of the geared limited-slip differential. It features a lifetime transferable warranty, even in race applications. Moser says that this is the only limited-slip differential that continues to drive in low- or no-traction situations, even if you have rear tire lift. Because it is geared, it is capable of handling 650 hp on street tires. (Photo Courtesy Moser Engineering)

Clutch-Type LSDs

Clutch and cone-type differentials are commonly installed in cars from the factory. In a clutch/cone differential, pressure rings on the clutch stack are forced outward as the pinion cross shaft tries to climb the ramps of the gear teeth. As the torque increases, more compression

Instead of clutches, the geared limited-slip differential is a "smart" differential. These units can transfer power from a slipping wheel to the wheel that has traction. Icy conditions sometimes require a little tap of the brakes to get both wheels under power. (Photo Courtesy Eaton)

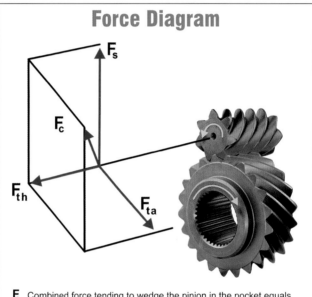

Force Diagram

F_c Combined force tending to wedge the pinion in the pocket equals

F_s Separating force due to pressure angle plus

F_{th} Thrust force due to helix angle plus

F_{ta} Tangential force between side gear and pinion

Geared limited-slip differentials operate via gear separation force. As differential rotating force is placed on the gears, such as that experienced during cornering, the gears climb out of mesh and are forced into pockets, allowing one axle to freewheel. As soon as torque is applied, the gear is pulled back and the gears become meshed, and the axles are once again engaged.

This Eaton limited-slip has been disassembled so you can see the component parts. The side gears are the larger gears; the spider gears are the small ones. The friction plates and metal spacer plates are in the center.

Spider gears are a key player in limited-slip differentials because they transfer torque to the side gears. Note the shape of the teeth themselves: Both sides are ramped but asymmetrical, a characteristic of a 1.5-type limited-slip differential.

The axles load into the splines on the side gears. The recess in the center is where the C-clip locks in. These are in good shape, without any significant wear, chips, or missing teeth.

A set of splines is on the backside of the side gear. The locking plate for the clutches engages these splines while the clutch plates are locked into the carrier housing. When the splines are engaged, the side gears turn the axles and then the wheels.

The spring pack is used to keep tension on the clutches. Most GM limited slips use four springs and two plates, but some use an S-spring. You can tune the level of slippage with the springs. Stock Eaton GM limited-slip differentials use 400-pound springs.

is put on the clutches, coupling the axles, and reducing slip; it functions similar to slipping the clutch on a manual transmission. The Eaton Posi (a clutch plate type) is the original Posi-Traction differential. It provides efficient transfer of power to the rear wheels equally so that acceleration is maximized yet controlled. Some of these units can be tuned with shims, different clutches, and even metal-on-metal clutches.

Clutch-type limited-slips are the most common and popular. Many owners opt for this differential because they are inexpensive compared to other limited-slip differentials and they deliver consistent performance for high-performance street cars. There are three different configurations: 1-, 1.5-, and 2-way. Each is suitable for a particular application; there are enough options to allow you to get the right style for your application.

The clutch-type LSD needs to be rebuilt after being subjected to extreme use and/or many miles because the clutch discs wear and have a limited service life. The clutch packs direct the torque to one wheel or the other. If worn, clutch packs are not rebuilt; the clutches eventually wear away and there is no coupling of the axles. This condition often exists in older muscle cars that have been driven hard for many years.

Replacing the clutches is not difficult, but you need to correctly break in the clutch pack. See "Project: Rebuilding a Clutch-Type Differential" on page 65). Each manufacturer has its own specific break-in procedures that must be followed to obtain optimum coupling. Although not difficult, the break-in is crucial. Another caveat to the clutch LSD is oil; all clutch LSDs require an LSD–gear oil additive.

Torque Application

The LSD operates on three input torque states: load, no load, and overrun. Under load, the axle coupling is in proportion to the torque load. Therefore, heavy torque loads yield full coupling while light torque yields a partial couple. Under no-load conditions, it operates in static couple similar to an open carrier. Overrun operation classifies the limited-slip type. Overrun is the sudden release of torque, such as hard on the throttle and then jumping off.

The manner in which the LSD reacts to overrun situations determines whether the LSD is a 1-, 1.5-, or 2-way. It's an important aspect for any street car.

The type of limited slip has a big impact on the driving characteristics of the vehicle. A 1-way LSD releases the coupling. The LSD releases the coupling as soon as the throttle lifts. This is the safest type of LSD, as it allows the rear tires to spin as needed.

It is a 2-way differential if it increases the coupling regardless of forward or reverse torque upon throttle release. Drift racers prefer the 2-way LSD, because it does

A stock Posi-Traction unit (right) compared to an aftermarket carrier (left) shows the strength of the aftermarket unit. The extra material on the case makes for a stronger carrier, with bigger gears and springs. This carrier is a Yukon clutch-type limited-slip differential.

The carrier has a pair of bearings on each side. The old bearings must be pressed off and new ones pressed on with a hydraulic press. If you don't have the right tools, take it to a machine shop. There are no shims or adjustments.

The center pin is another potential failure point for the carrier. In this case, this pin broke around the locking-bolt hole, allowing it to slide out. Luckily, the driver was just barely rolling and the differential was not under an enormous load, otherwise much more damage could have been done. When the pin came out, it locked up the differential. This could have split the case of the housing if it had happened at speed.

Some aftermarket carriers eliminate the center pin altogether. This Eaton Truetrac uses a solid plug design. The C-clips are installed first.

not open the coupling when the driver lets off the gas, going from 100- to 0-percent throttle. This does two things: It allows the driver to be in control of the wheel spin, the differential is engaged, and in terms of drifting, it keeps the wheels spinning throughout the drift. However, an inexperienced driver can fall into an unwanted spin with a 2-way LSD.

The middle ground is the 1.5, which has less deceleration lock-up than the 2-way but retains the coupling, unlike the 1-way.

Most performance applications should consider a 1.5- or 2-way unit to maintain vehicle control. Road

course, auto-crossing and aggressive street driving are best suited for a 1.5-LSD. The 2-way differentials remain in a hard lock during aggressive cornering. Drift racers and experienced road racers often use a 2-way LSD, but these drivers have the experience and skill to control the car with a 2-way on the limit. A 2-way should only be used by a skilled and experienced driver on the street, otherwise its use can lead to loss of control; many drivers find the 2-way differentials challenging. Imagine turning a corner with your foot deep in the throttle. As the axle assembly breaks away and the vehicle goes into over-

steer, you let off the gas.

A 1.5- or 1-way differential allows the spinning tires to slow as needed, but a 2-way remains in a hard lock, making it much more difficult to control the slide.

Ramp Shape

The shape of the ramp on the spider gears determines the LSD type. The spider gears climb the side gears as the carrier spins in the case. The ramp of each gear tooth controls how the rotational torque is applied. Under load, the drive-side of the gear is climbing the front edge of the side gear teeth, controlling the clutches.

When torque is suddenly removed, the backside of the gears takes over as the side gears are running up on the back of the spider gear teeth.

If both ramps of the gear teeth have symmetrical slopes, the differential is a 2-way. If they look like saw-teeth (one vertical, one sloped) then the LSD is a 1-way. If both sides have sloped ramps but are asymmetrical, it is a 1.5-way differential. A 1-way LSD has the quietest, smoothest, most noise-free operation. The 2-way tends to be a little noisy, the cut of the gears and increased clutch pressure tend to "chirp" around corners. This is not tire chirp, but rather the clutches slipping.

The differential pin shattered into several small pieces. A small piece of the pin was lying in the bottom of the car. The center pin bolt held the carrier together for a while, but the pin had been broken for a fairly long time. The carrier was actually undamaged and can be reused.

Project: Installing Plug and Separator Block

1 Install Plug and Separator

This plug and separator block for the Eaton Truetrac is also used for the Eaton Detroit Locker; it is much stronger than stock. The separator block installs between the axles, and provides much better reliability than the stock pin, especially in high-horsepower applications. These typically do not back out or break.

2 Install Snap Ring

Place the plug in the carrier (it goes in easily) and use snap ring pliers to place the snap ring into the retention groove in the carrier.

3 Install Snap Ring (CONTINUED)

Important!

Make sure the snap ring is fully seated. If it comes out, the axle will suffer substantial damage.

4 Separate Ring Gear and Carrier

In most cases, this step is fairly easy, but sometimes it takes a bit of effort, especially if the gears have been on the carrier for years. You can lightly tap the gear to break it free from the carrier. Tap the gear in several places until you have a slight gap between the gear and the carrier.

---

5 Separate Ring Gear and Carrier (CONTINUED)

Once there is some room between the carrier and ring gear, you can insert a prybar, but be careful when you use it because you don't want to damage the carrier or the ring gear. If you have a soft vise, you can put the assembly in it. Otherwise, having a second set of hands to support the gear is a good idea.

6 Inspect New Gear

Inspect the new ring gear for any signs of damage, burrs, or problems in the casting. You should also clean off the shipping grease. The new gear should slide on nice and easy.

7 Bolt Carrier to Ring Gear

Place the carrier against the ring gear and thread two bolts into the back of the ring gear at opposite sides of the gear. You just need them finger tight so the ring gear and carrier are attached. This allows you to hang the ring gear upside down.

8 Install Carrier Bolts

Apply red Loctite or another high-strength thread locker to the bolt threads. Thread them into the ring gear but do not torque them down yet.

Torque Fasteners

9 Install Carrier bolts (CONTINUED)

Tighten the bolts in a star-pattern and then torque them to spec. For GM differentials, 55 to 65 ft-lbs is the general rule. You will need a helper for this task.

Project: Installing Ladder Bars

When it comes to building a street/strip drag car, you need to make some compromises. Big power coupled with a stiff chassis and stock leaf springs is a recipe for no traction. Leaf springs, like traction bars and installing stiffer springs, offer a Band-Aid fix. But the inherent problem remains; there is no static connection to the chassis. The axle assembly is hanging off the chassis on a stack of steel leaf springs that shift, twist, and wrap up. This allows the tire to leave the payment so traction and control are compromised. In addition, the leaf springs sit outside the subframe rails, seriously cutting into the wheel well area. Because I am running slicks on the Royal Scamp, I need a better solution.

Suspension Choices

In addition to independent rear suspensions, you can choose a leaf spring, ladder bar, or four-link suspension. Leaf spring rear suspensions perform well for some applications, but a serious drag car doesn't use the stock leaf springs. Instead, most drag cars use a four-link–style suspension because it offers the maximum amount of adjustability and allows for chassis tuning at the track.

The four-link uses an upper and lower bar on each side that connects the chassis to the rear end. These may run parallel or be triangulated. The top bars run outward from the center of the chassis to the rear. The bars connect to the chassis and rear via rod ends that bolt to plates. These plates typically have 8 to 12 potential mounting points so there are quite a few tuning options.

The ladder bar suspension provides adjustability on the front side (bar to chassis) and a static mount to the rear. For the novice, ladder bars are easier to tune than the four-link, and when set up correctly, they provide the same benefits. As with the four-link, ladder bars use a coil-over shock to support the weight of the vehicle. This also allows for more tuning, such as ride height; with adjustable shocks, the dampening factor can be tuned.

Beyond tuning, the thing that makes ladder bars (and the four-link) so effective is the controlled motion of the suspension arc. The motion through the range of travel occurs the same way, every time. This static connection to the chassis controls wheel hop and promotes better weight transfer to the tires for optimum traction. Leaf springs simply cannot do this; there are too many variables. What one side does can differ from what the other side does. The choice for the Royal Scamp is ladder bars.

Shocks

Installing ladder bars is a big task. Although a few bolt-in kits are available, most kits are weld-on systems. I chose a 36-inch ladder bar for a custom drag car from Chris Alston's ChassisWorks. The kit came with the ladder bars, coil-over shocks, track locater, and tubing for mounting the system. I went with VariShock double-adjustable shocks for maximum tuning. I could have installed 32-inch bars, which would have pulled the front crossmember rearward about 4 inches (this would have put it on the factory subframe), but the longer bars provide more stability and because I was adding subframe connectors, it was not a problem.

The rear coil-over mounts are one key area that added difficulty to this project. Factory shock mounts are typically not suitable for supporting the entire back end of the car. The shocks have a maximum extended length of 14 inches, and minimum travel of 13 inches. The recommended travel is right in the middle at 13.5 inches.

With this setup, I need to mock up a set of shocks. With the rear ride height of 10 inches and the shock mounted in the middle of the shock mount, the top of the shock mount was above the stock floor. I could have dropped it down, but would have lost some adjustability. The shock crossmember was welded to the rear down-bars on the roll cage. This might not be acceptable for some builders, so choose your shocks and springs carefully. A shorter 10-inch spring and matching shock would probably fit under the stock floor, but take your own measurements first.

Results

It took about a month to get it all together, which was mostly evenings and weekends, including all the measuring and cutting out the floors. There is probably 100 hours' worth of work on this project.

With a set of Toyo 12-inch slicks mounted to 15 x 10 centerline "Fuel" drag wheels, I had about an inch of clearance on either side (stock frame rail to the outer wheel well lip). Gaining this much room is worth the effort of the swap, not to mention the superior traction.

You must take your time and measure five times. This is one area where you don't want to rush things.

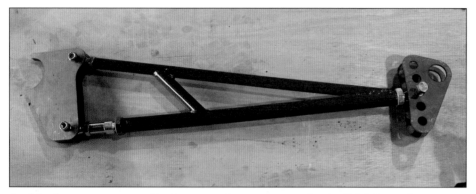

Ladder bars are an excellent suspension accessory for both high-performance vehicles and off-roaders because they help anchor the axle for improved traction and performance. In addition, they offer excellent articulation and the ability to tune the suspension.

1 Install Threaded Rod Ends

Thread the tie-rod end into the ladder bar. Thread each end 3/4 of the way so you can adjust it once it is hung on the suspension.

2 Measure for Fitment

You can use a sheet of plywood on the floor for protection when you assemble the bars. Square the bars 90 degrees to the vertical center of the rear differential mounting point and measure the actual length of the bars. The long bar with the rod end fully threaded is the upper bar. It is important to ensure that the bars are located correctly front to back in the wheel well.

3 Measure Suspension Arms

During the mockup, check where the bars should sit at ride height, which is 8 inches from the axle centerline to the top of the wheel arch, providing 12 inches of ground clearance. The lower portion of the bar (the long side) should rest parallel to the ground at ride height. Using a magnetic level, the lower bar should read close to 0, or 90 degrees. If the 0 is on the top, the needle should point to 90. If 90 is at the top, the needle should point to 0. Also measure and mark the wheel center-to-front ladder bar mounting point at ride height.

4 Measure Subframe Connector Mounting Points

You marked the subframe connector at 38 inches. Double-check the mark with a measuring tape. The overall length of the ladder bars, including the mounting brackets, to the center of the forward crossmember mount is 38 inches.

5 Locate Front Mounting Points

Once you are satisfied with the position of the ladder bars use the front ladder bar brackets to mark the subframe. With the bracket rotated so that the pick-up points run 90 degrees to the ground (straight up and down), and the upper edge just touching the floor, mark the subframe connector with a half-moon. You will weld in a round crossmember here. Note the roll cage tube coming through the floor; you will tie it to the crossmember tube for extra stiffness.

6 Cut Frame Rails for Front Mounting Brackets

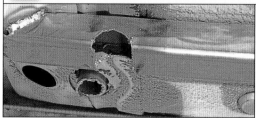

Trim the rails with a plasma torch because cutting half-moons with a hole saw is difficult with the connectors on the car. Dress the cuts with a right-angle grinder and grinding disc.

Precision Measurement

7 Measure Ride Height

Use the adjustable rear end from Chapter 2 to set the height of the car. Measure both the vertical wheel centerline and the ride height using the center of the wheel well arch (which you marked for the original centerline before removing the original rear), and the lower quarter panel in front of the wheel. This unique device allowed you to mount the wheels and set the width of the rear end so you could narrow the housing.

8 Measure for Position of Front Mounts

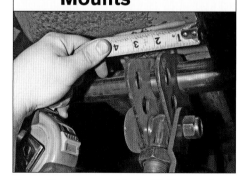

Once the rear end is built, the real work begins. Hold the ladder bar crossmember in the car with jack stands and set the position of the mounts. Measure 2 inches from the inner side of the subframe connectors to the outer mount. Bolt the ladder bar rod ends in place to keep everything lined up.

9 Tack Weld Front Mounting Brackets in Position

Use a MIG welder to place the front mounting brackets under the car. Complete only one side; the other side must match, and that comes later. Mark the for location in the subframe.

10 Weld Crossmember

Remove the entire crossmember and fully weld the brackets with a single bead. The outside and inside edges of the brackets should be welded up.

11 Assemble Crossmember

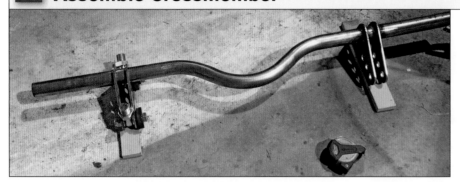

Assemble the mounts for the other bar (inner and outer ladder bar mounts and the rod ends for each, bolted together) in the same manner. Place the entire assembly on the floor. The fully welded side ensures the correct geometry for the unwelded side. Measure each side to ensure the opposite mounts are in the right place. Nice and simple.

12 Weld Crossmember to Chassis

Reset the crossmember into the car, aligned to the original marks. Measure for correct placement, and then weld in place.

13 Install Rod Ends on Bracket

Reinstall the rod ends into the bars (with antisieze!) and bolt them in place. Set the ride height to the center position so you have some adjustment room. You will torque them down when the final assembly is on the ground.

14 Weld Rear Mounts to Axle Assembly

Install the rear end mounts and place them up to the rear housing. The optimal position for the rear end is 2 to 3 degrees down angle to the front of the car. This provides the right geometry for the driveshaft rotation. A magnetic angle protractor is really helpful for this project.

15 Weld Rear Mounts to Axle Assembly (CONTINUED)

Tack weld the ladder bar mounts and the shock mounts in place. You can put the shock mounts anywhere, but the farther apart, the better. You can keep it simple and place them between the ladder bar mounts.

16 Weld Rear Mounts to Axle Assembly (CONTINUED)

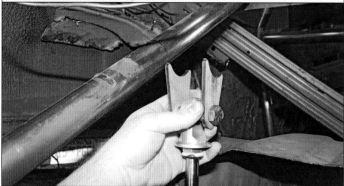

Assemble the shocks (no springs yet) and bolt them to the lower mount. Position the upper mount ears vertically and mark the placement for the crossmember.

17 Measure Rear Down Bars

Measure the distance between the two rear down bars of the cage and transfer it to the 1⅝-inch-diameter tubing supplied for the shock crossmember. Take the measurement between the two down bars. You can use a PipeMaster notching helper to get the right shape for the notches, and then install the tube between the down bars.

18 Weld Rear Shock Mounts

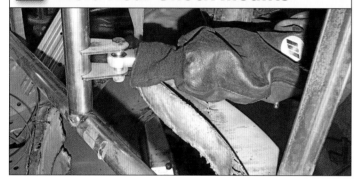

Slide one of the Miller welding sleeves over the shock to protect it and position the ears to the crossmember. The placement is not critical, so you can position the shock so that the lower shock mount is centered between the ladder bar mounts on the housing. It is always best to set the shocks as close to vertical as possible. Then weld the tabs in place.

19 Assemble Shocks

Remove the shocks from the upper mounts and install the springs. Assembling the shocks is a little tricky. You may have to use a set of spring compressors to get the upper retainer in place, even with the lower retainer threaded all the way down.

20 Bolt Lower Shock Mount to Brackets

Bolt the shocks to the lower shock mount using the supplied hardware and spacers. The ride height can be adjusted later using the threaded lower retainer on the shock.

21 Bolt Upper Shock Mount to Crossmember

With the shocks in place, tack weld the lower shock mount to the housing. All that is left is to pull the rear end and finish welding the brackets in place.

22 Mount Track Locator Bar

This bar centers the rear housing under the car. You can use a panhard bar, track locator, or Watt's linkage. The track locator bolts to opposing sides (one front and one rear) for the ladder bar mounting bolts with rod ends. Turning the rod moves the rear to the left or right depending on your needs.

Torque and Horsepower Capacity

The amount of power a unit can transmit depends on a lot of variables including size (10- or 12-bolt), manufacturer, tires, and intended use. For instance, a factory street clutch LSD can handle more power on the street with radial street tires than it can on a track with drag slicks. A stock clutch-type LSD can transmit 350 to 400 hp on the street. The Eaton Truetrac gear-type unit is capable of handling 650 hp in the same situation. With some prep work, a clutch-type LSD can handle a 9-second Buick Grand National that lifts the front wheels for 100 feet.

Be sure to research the manufacturer's recommended power specs for each application.

Clutch-Type Differentials

General Motors has several names for its limited-slip differential unit. Commonly referred to as Posi-Traction, the exact same clutch-based LSD is also called Controlled Traction, Saf-T-Grip, and Positive Traction. This is a clutch-type LSD. That means a stack of clutch discs are packed together to provide the grip.

In the standard pack, there are nine clutches per side: five locking discs with tabs on the outer side that lock into the case and four discs that are splined to lock onto the side gears. When the spider gears pressurize the side gears, the clutch packs press together, providing the positive coupling of the axles. Because the unit uses clutches, they eventually wear out, essentially becoming an open-type differential.

Most of the factory clutch-type LSD units are based on the Eaton LSD, which means that the parts interchange across several brands and sizes. The clutches for the GM 10-bolt (8.2- and 8.5-inch) and both car and truck 12-bolt LSD units are exactly the same as the Ford 9- and 8.8-inch, and the Chrysler 8¾, making parts readily available.

Steel Clutch Packs

Four clutch pack options are available. Most stock LSD units use an 18-disc clutch pack, with 9 discs per side. These solid discs use high-quality steel with crosshatched lines on both sides. This is the friction surface, which is metal-on-metal. These do wear out, but it takes a long time for that to happen. Unless the steel discs are severely worn, you can shim the clutch pack to increase the pressure on the discs, regaining the limited-slip action. These discs are very strong and don't break, but they tend to chatter, especially with the heavier center springs.

The GM service kit uses an 18-disc pack with a series of slots cut around the perimeter of the clutch discs. These slots reduce chatter, but they end up weakening the disc, which leads to breakage. In addition, they still chatter when used with 400- and 800-pound springs. Most builders prefer the solid discs.

For race cars, the Eaton 22-disc clutch pack is available. These clutches work well in extreme conditions, until the locking tabs on the intermediate discs wear out. These discs chatter with all spring combinations and require frequent service.

Eaton also makes a carbon-fiber clutch kit for LSD units. It is a 14-disc pack with seven per side, and uses a more traditional fiber-clutch and steel-plate configuration. Each of the three clutch discs has a carbon-fiber pad on either side that engages the smooth steel surface of the intermediate discs. In this pack, the clutches have tabs that lock into the case on the side, and the intermediate discs lock onto the side gear. The carbon-fiber material provides excellent grip without chattering when used with 400-pound springs or less.

Spring Rates

Four spring rates are available for Eaton clutch-type LSD units: 200, 300, 400, and 800 pounds, which indicates the preload on the clutches. These spring kits are available from Eaton or General Motors. For most street performance vehicles, the 400-pound springs are best. The 800-pound springs are very tight and produce more chatter and less slip in the corners. All Eaton Posi units come from the factory with 400-pound springs.

Project: Rebuilding a Clutch-Type Limited-Slip Differential

Rebuilding a clutch-type differential is not difficult, but it does require some patience. You need to use spring compressor or sliding clamps, the proper wrenches, and other materials. To properly assemble the clutch-type limited-slip differential, carefully perform the following procedures.

Disassembly

For rebuilding a clutch-type differential, the first step is to remove the carrier from the vehicle. In most cases, the cross shaft is already out. However, in vehicles with bolt-in axles, you have to remove the cross shaft first.

You must secure the housing in a bench vise and the rest of the process can be done on the workbench. Place the ring gear pad in the vise and clamp it down, with the large hole in the case facing up. The springs and plates must be removed first. Using a pry bar or screwdriver, gently pry on the plates to slide them out of the housing.

As the assembly begins to come out, use a clamp to keep tension on the springs; otherwise, they will fly everywhere. You can release the tension slowly once the assembly is fully removed from the housing, or keep them together.

1 Remove Spring Plates

Before you start, place the differential in a soft vise so it's firmly anchored to the bench and easy to work on. Rebuilding a clutch-type limited-slip differential is not difficult, but you do need to follow some specific procedures. First, carefully remove the spring plates with a screwdriver or prybar. Don't pry too hard on the springs, if they come out of the plates, they can bounce anywhere. Work the plates out evenly, walking them out side to side.

2 Compress Clutch Plates

Once you have pried up the clutch plates until the edges are exposed, use soft wood Irwin clamps or C-clamps to grab the edge of the plates and compress the plates. The springs place tension on the plate and if not compressed, they will fly all over the workshop when removed from the differential.

3 Remove Spider Gears

Slowly roll the spider gears by hand and remove them by hand from the case. If it has a thrust washer, keep it with its gear. You roll out each gear separately.

4 Remove Side Gears

With the spider gears out of the case, simply lift out the side gears. Remember how the keepers slide out of the case. There are a total of four keepers.

5 Inspect Parts

Be sure to inspect the clutch plates, side gears, spider gears, and all other miscellaneous parts. In this particular case, the gears in the set were good; just a new set of clutches was in order.

6 Inspect Side Gears

The side gears are the last part of the clutch pack. Inspect the inner surface for hot spots, pitting, or bluing. If you have any of these issues, replace the side gears.

7 Inspect Steel Plates

Stock clutches use steel plates with crosshatches on them. Although these clutches are not in bad shape, the housing had a lot of metal shavings in the oil and they were a little loose in the pack. These clutches don't wear very much and can often be reused with a shim pack. If the discs have discoloration, they need to be replaced. You might want to change the stock discs to carbon-fiber clutches anyway.

The spider gears and side gears work together in mesh, so you need to spin them to get them out. Rotate the side gears until the spider gears reach the large hole and remove them. You have to rotate the side gears twice, as the one spider works its way 180 degrees from the hole.

With the spider gears out, the side gears slide right out of the case. Be mindful of the locking clip that holds the discs in the slot. There are two clips per side. Most rebuild kits come with replacement clips, but if you are just shimming your LSD, you need to keep them.

At this point, you should have all of the main components out of the case and on the bench. Remove the clutch packs from the side gears, and pay attention to how they are positioned on the gear, including the shims between the pack and the side gear. Keep this arrangement side to side.

Parts Inspection

Be sure to inspect the gears for excessive wear and any obvious damage. They should be smooth, without any chips, missing teeth, or rough patches. The spider gears should have smooth, shiny surfaces where they ride in the case and should not be pitted or discolored. The side gears should be clean and free of chips, scarring, or missing teeth.

Also inspect the inner splines for the axles and the outer splines for the clutches for damage.

The clutches should be intact, with no breaks, cracks, or discoloration. If you are reusing the clutches, make sure that the crosshatches are uniform and not significantly worn. If you are replacing the clutches, this inspection is not critical. Look at the case for obvious signs of wear. Replace any part that is suspect.

Clutch Pack Assembly

The clutch plates and wearable discs assemble in a specific sequence. From the inside of the side gear the sequence is: locking disc, spline disc, locking disc, spline disc, and so on until the pack is fully stacked and topped off with the original shims.

The number of discs varies by the style of clutch. For carbon-fiber clutches, the clutch material is on the locking disc, with the splined disc between. The stack sequence is the same.

These clutches are the wet type, meaning that they need to be lubricated. Apply new gear oil to each disc, including the inner side gear surface, before stacking the pack.

1 Unpack Clutch Rebuild Kit

Limited-slip clutch plates are made from a variety of materials, including steel and carbon fiber. Aftermarket replacements are available in several versions. Yukon Gear offers this 14-disc pack with carbon-fiber clutches for about $250; it includes all of the clutch discs and new retainer clips.

2 Inspect Clutch Plates

The carbon fiber clutches provide ample grip and excellent torque transfer while maintaining a long life span. The steels between the clutches are new to match the clutches. Before you go ahead and install the parts, carefully look over the mating surfaces and tabs. Although these are brand-new parts, problems in packing and manufacturing can occur. You need to ensure the parts are not damaged.

3 Clean Clutch Plates

Spray brake cleaner over the new clutch discs to strip away any shipping grease.

4 Prelube Clutch Parts

Prelube all of the parts, including the clutches, with a product such as Royal Purple gear oil. Spread the oil onto the parts with your fingers. Synthetic oil is just fine for breaking in a differential but don't use it for an engine build.

Gear Installation

Once the clutch pack is assembled, the clutch pack and other parts can be installed in the differential housing. The side gears are fairly simple, but the locking tabs can fall off easily. Dab a bit of grease on the locking clip to hold them in place.

The spider gears are tricky. You have to compress the packs on both sides and spin the side gears at the same time. There is not much room for two sets of hands, so you will have to improvise. If

you have a spreader clamp, use it. I use a bolt with a coupling nut to spread the load across the gears.

Place the spider gear in the housing and roll the gears until it is in the 180-degree location below the large opening. Reset your spreader device and place the other spider gear into the housing. If you have it just right, the two gears should line up with the cross-shaft holes. If you are a tooth off, you have to start over. Once the gears are aligned, reinstall the spring pack along with the cross shaft.

1 Place Clutch Disc on Side Gear

To begin the clutch pack assembly process, place all 14 discs in the correct order on the side gear. Place the clutch disc onto the side gear. Each clutch kit comes with specific instructions for stacking the pack.

2 Place Locking Disc on Clutch Disc

Place the locking disc over the clutch disc.

3 Coat with Oil

Make sure each side of the splined locking disc is coated with gear oil.

4 Coat with Oil (CONTINUED)

Make sure to spread the assembly lube across the face of the disc. Repeat the process with the rest of the clutch pack.

5 Add Keepers

When all of the discs are loaded, place the keepers onto the clutch stack. It may help to add a dab of moly grease to hold them in place.

6 Install Pack in Carrier

Now that you have a fully assembled clutch pack, install it in the case. Carefully lower the side gear pack into the carrier, making sure that all discs remain in place. This part of the procedure can be tricky because the keepers tend to fall off. A dab of moly grease might help keep them in place.

7 Roll in First Side Gear

Once both side gears have been installed in the differential housing, roll the first spider gear into the case by spinning one of the side gears. It has to be rolled into the position on the gears.

8 Roll in First Side Gear (CONTINUED)

A spacer such as this one (made from a 1/4-inch bolt and coupler nut) helps push the side gears into the case so the other side gear can be installed. As you install the other spider gear, the side gears become tighter in the case.

9 Roll in First Side Gear (CONTINUED)

Using the axle to spin the side gear helps roll the side gear into place. The clutches are very tight, so the added torque is helpful.

10 Place Second Side Gear

You may have to experiment with a few pry tools to get the second gear into place. Using the center pin to stake the first spider is a good idea. The side gears become tight and spinning them is tricky. If the spider gear is off even one tooth, it doesn't line up with the center pin. Be patient, you will get it.

11 Place Second Side Gear (CONTINUED)

Drop the second gear into place and spin the side gear with the axle shaft to move it into position. The axle shaft makes it much easier to spin the side gear and roll the spider gear into position. It may take a few tries to position the spider correctly.

12 Align Side Gears

Getting the two side gears into alignment with the center pin holes can be frustrating, but with some patience it will eventually line up. If the gear is off, remove it and spin it one tooth up or down on the side gear and try again.

Testing the Differential

At this stage, you can test the operation of your differential. You can use the axle shaft to engage one side gear and spin it or clamp the axle into the vise and rotate the housing. To do this, you need a bench and vise. If the housing spins easily, the clutch packs are not engaging and the limited-slip is not functioning. Thus, you need to add more shims to the clutch pack; try to add shims equally per side, one at a time. If it is tight, and requires a lot of effort to spin, it should be good. This is the method most builders use.

The spider gear clearance can also change how the unit locks up. Either steel or brass shims are available to tighten the spider gears. If your unit had shims between the case and the spider gear, reuse them. If the gears are not tight to the side gears, you can use a thicker shim. The goal is to have a nice, tight differential; if there is any play or it spins easily, add shims.

Axle Assembly Continues

In this chapter, I have explained how to rebuild the Chevy 12-bolt differential carrier. Specifically, I have detailed the steps for assembling the clutch pack and installing the clutch pack in the carrier. Before you install the carrier in the differential housing, refer to the installation of the pinion gear in Chapter 8. There, I reveal how to install the pinion gear and set it at the correct depth in the case. The pinion bearing, seal, and yoke installations are also detailed in Chapter 8. After the carrier has been installed, you need to check ring and pinion gear mesh, which is also specified in Chapter 8. When backlash has been determined and is within spec, you're close to completing the entire axle assembly so follow the remainder of the procedures in Chapter 8.

GEARS

Selecting the correct hypoid gears for your vehicle and application is essential for attaining maximum performance. The gears are shaped as a revolved hyperboloid, which means that the pitch surface of the gear itself is a hyperbolic surface. Hypoid gears are centered off-axis, where the pinion gear sits lower than the centerline of the ring gear, allowing the pinion gear to be larger than it would be if it were on-center. Because of the size and spiral angle of the pinion gear, hypoids engage multiple teeth at once, so they can handle higher torque loads.

One of the side effects of the hypoid design is a sliding action of the gear teeth as they rotate. This is where a lot of issues appear. As the teeth slide along each other, the friction generates heat, which is the enemy of gears. If a differential runs low on gear oil for even a short time it results in serious damage so that it is unrepairable; you have to replace the gears.

The gears must be arranged in a very specific position relative to each other, within a couple of thousandths of mesh. This is expressed numerically as .002 inch, which is similar to the bearing clearances in the rotating assembly of an engine. The problem is that while it is easy to measure the clearance between a crankshaft journal and a rod, doing the same on a ring gear set is much more difficult. See Chapter 7 for more details.

Determine Gear Ratio

Determining the ratio of gears installed inside your housing is simple. You need to count the rotations of the tires and the driveshaft at the same time. It is easiest with a helper, but you can do it alone with some preparation. First, you need a floor jack, jackstands, tape or a grease marker, as well as paper and a pen.

Jack the vehicle up until the wheels are suspended. Secure the jackstands under the vehicle and rest the weight of the car on the stands. (*Never* work under a car with just a floor jack. If the floor jack fails, you can be severely injured.) Place a piece of tape from the fender to the tire or to the ground and to the tire along the sidewall. This is the rotational marker. Place another piece of

Ring gears convert the engine's rotation into forward motion, but there is more to selecting a gear set than just what size you think you need.

A sizing code is stamped on every pinion shaft. Gears are built as a matched set, and they cannot be interchanged.

The number of teeth is stamped on each gear. The small number is the pinion gear tooth count; the large number is the ring gear tooth count. You divide the big number by the little number to get the ratio. Here, 40 ÷ 13 = 3.076, so these are 3.08:1 gears.

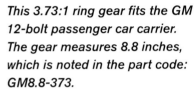

This 3.73:1 ring gear fits the GM 12-bolt passenger car carrier. The gear measures 8.8 inches, which is noted in the part code: GM8.8-373.

To change gear ratios, you need different pinion gear sizes. This pinion gear (left) is a 4.11, and the gear (right) is a 3.08. This is part of the reason that different carriers are required for certain gear ranges. The bigger the gear ratio, the farther away the pinion gear sits. The carrier repositions the ring gear to compensate.

tape from the driveshaft to the housing. This is the driveshaft marker. If you are working by yourself, you can put the tire marker on the inside of the tire so you can see it from under the car.

Put the transmission in neutral. Next, rotate the driveshaft and count the number of complete rotations until the tire has made one full revolution. It is unlikely that the driveshaft rotations will be equal, so you can approximate the number for a street vehicle. About 3/4 of a turn gets you close to .73 to .80. This is good enough for street vehicles.

If you need a more precise indication of the gear ratio, open the housing and read the numbers stamped into the each gear. If you can't read the numbers, simply count the teeth and use the following formula:

Gear Ratio = ring teeth ÷ pinion teeth

For example, a vehicle with 39 ring teeth and 11 pinion teeth has a 3.54:1 gear ratio (39 ÷ 11). The gears' purpose is to transfer power from the engine to the wheels, and the differential does this by torque multiplication. If an engine were directly connected to the wheels, the vehicle would struggle to move. The enormous size and resistance of the wheel would overload the engine and bog it down. The vehicle would take a long time to actually move.

During acceleration, the engine is spinning from idle (650 to 1,000 rpm) to the 5,000-rpm range for normal street driving. Forward motion begins almost instantly without reducing the engine's speed. This is because of torque multiplication: As torque increases, the speed of rotation decreases. The basic formulas are:

Ring Gear Torque = input torque x axle ratio

Ring Gear Speed = input speed ÷ axle ratio

For example, a stock LS1 engine sends 345 ft-lbs of torque to a rear differential with 3.73:1 gears at 4,400 rpm. An engine that produces

Anatomy of a Ring Gear

Check the pattern of the mesh at the ring gear to verify final setup of the gears. To confirm that the final setup is correct, you need to know the details of the nomenclature. You must know several key areas: coast, drive, heel, toe, face (or crown), and flank (or root).

Checking the patterns on the gear mesh requires being able to "read" the gears themselves.

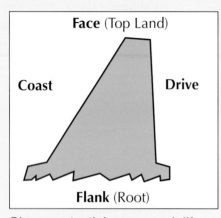

Face (Top Land)

Coast   **Drive**

Flank (Root)

Ring gear teeth have several different areas, or aspects, that serve different operations. You need to understand the nomenclature for the gear teeth so you can evaluate the mesh. The long side is the "coast" side and the gears mesh when no power is delivered. The vertical side is the "drive" side and, therefore, as power is applied the teeth of the pinion and ring gear mesh. The top, or face, is called the top land, and the base is called the root, or flank.

On this typical ring gear for a Chevy 12-bolt, you can see the various components of the gears. The inside of the ring gear is called the toe and the outside is called the heel.

The pointer is showing the top land. You need to carefully examine your old gears for chips along this surface. High-mileage or worn ring gears often show wear or damage in this area.

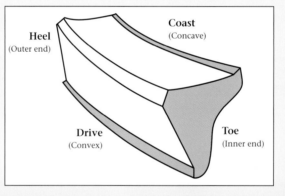

Heel
(Outer end)

Coast
(Concave)

Drive
(Convex)

Toe
(Inner end)

This diagram shows the convex/concave shape of the gear teeth.

When setting up used gears you need to focus attention on the coast side because the drive side has a wear pattern already established. You cannot change a wear pattern once it is set.

Most of the force on the gears occurs on the drive side. When setting up a new gear set, be sure that the mesh is clean and centered. If the mesh is incorrect, the ring and pinion will prematurely wear out and generate gear whine.

You never want to find broken ring gear teeth but this kind of damage is somewhat common. Too much torque for the gear set, wear, and contaminants in the gear oil can chip ring gear teeth. In some cases, a foreign particle can become wedged in the gear and cause it to sheer off.

Coast

Coast is the freewheel side (or the backside) of the gear. This is where the two gears mesh when the vehicle is coasting. The coast side of the gear is concave from heel to toe, meaning that it curves into the center like the inside of a bowl.

Drive

The drive side of the gear is the most important in terms of mesh. On the drive side, the gears contact each other under acceleration or drive. The drive side is convex from heel to toe, meaning that it bulges at the center like the outside of a bowl.

Heel

The gears on a ring have an arc, and the outer circumference of the ring is the heel side.

Toe

The opposite of the heel is the inner side of the tooth, which is the toe. This is toward the center of the carrier.

Face

This is the top of the tooth itself; also referred to as the crown or top land.

Flank

The base of the gear is called the flank or root, which is the bulk of the gear itself. ∎

---

345 ft-lbs certainly has respectable torque, but it is simply not enough to get a 4,000-pound vehicle moving.

You can test this on a vehicle with a manual transmission. Start out in first gear, and the vehicle takes off like normal; start off in fourth, and the engine bogs down and dies. This is because it takes tremendous torque to generate forward motion. Using the formulas you get 1,287 ft-lbs of torque (345 x 3.73) and 1,180 rpm (4,400 ÷ 3.73).

As a result of these increases, the mechanical advantage of the drivetrain as a whole has increased. However, the axle assembly is only one component of the drivetrain; and there is always a second set of gears in the drivetrain: the transmission.

To get the complete picture, you need the vehicle's gearing. For example, an LS1 transmission with 350 hp and 345 ft-lbs of torque, is a Tremec T56 6-speed with the following gearing numbers:

First	2.97
Second	2.07
Third	1.43
Fourth	1.00
Fifth	.84
Sixth	.56

As an example, the rear differential is fitted with 3.73:1 gears. Using the formula, the final torque output at peak RPM in first gear is 3,822 ft-lbs (345 x 2.97 x 3.73). Total RPM is 397 (4,400 ÷ 2.97 ÷ 3.73).

This means that by the time the engine is spinning at 4,400 rpm, the axles are seeing 3,822 ft-lbs of rotational torque, spinning just 397 times per minute. This would certainly get a 4,000-pound car moving down the road.

Shift the transmission into fourth, and the gearing of the transmission is 1:1, so the torque and RPM of the transmission is exactly the same as the engine (minus a little bit for parasitic loss). The first calculation determines the torque needed from the gears, just 1,287 ft-lbs, to move the car.

An object in motion tends to stay in motion. Once the vehicle is in motion, the torque required to keep it in motion is drastically reduced, and when the vehicle is in motion, horsepower takes over. Torque gets the vehicle moving and horsepower keeps it moving at speed. Consider the example vehicle in sixth gear; plugging the data into the formulas you get 721 ft-lbs of final torque

---

(345 x .56 x 3.73) at 4,400 rpm and 165 rpm (345 ÷ .56 ÷ 3.73). There is very little output in terms of torque and rotational speed, yet the vehicle would be traveling at a very high rate of speed.

This is important because there are trade-offs for gear ratios and the way they relate to vehicle acceleration (quickness) and overall speed (speed). For a gear to achieve more mechanical advantage (numerically higher ratio), the pinion gear has to become smaller. Not only does this make the gear weaker, it also limits the top speed of the vehicle.

Gear Selection

A variety of terms can be used to describe gear type, such as "short," "deep," "tall," or "highway." These terms typically lead to confusion even for an experienced car owner/mechanic. Short gears are numerically higher, such as 3.73:1 or 4.11:1 ratios. These are the deep gears that get the vehicle moving quickly due to their high ratio of input to output rotations.

Tall or highway gears are the low-number ratios that yield high speed and efficiency, such as 2.80:1 or 3.08:1. These gears do not provide the torque multiplication rates that the larger ratios provide. Once the vehicle is up to speed, they allow the engine to spin more slowly, which means they are more efficient for highway use.

Finding the ratio is simple. For every rotation of the ring gear, the pinion gear rotates "X.XX" times. For example, a 3.73:1 gear set requires 3.73 turns of the pinion gear to spin the ring gear one full rotation. This is a direct correlation of the driveshaft rotation to the axle rotation. The lower the number, the faster the axles

spin in relation to the engine. This is why lower gears are efficient; the engine doesn't have to spin as fast to keep the car moving and can reach higher speed, but it is much harder to get the car going than with larger numerical gears.

Choosing the gear ratio for your vehicle can be difficult. You have to find the balance between top speed and quickness for your application. Specific applications, such as drag racers and off-road rock crawlers need deep gears to get the vehicle moving quickly or maximize engine torque output at low speeds. High-speed racing, such as with circle track cars, needs top-end speed, so the takeoff speed is not much of a factor.

Street vehicles, however, must strike a fine balance between the two, and that means factoring in several key components such as intended use, transmission type and gearing, and tires.

Intended Use

This is the single most important component for gear selection. If you are building a stoplight-to-stoplight street machine, higher numerical gears are certainly applicable. If the vehicle sees a lot of highway miles, steep gears drastically reduce the overall speed of the vehicle and make the engine spin much faster.

Transmission Type and Gearing

The following gear ratio setup is one of the greatest upgrades for a transmission overdrive. It does the opposite of the lower gears; it makes the output shaft spin *faster* than the engine itself. This means that the rear gears have more input speed to work with. A 1:1 transmission with output running to a 3.73:1 rear gear yields a 3.73:1 final drive; a .68 over-

drive yields a 2.54:1 final drive. This is like having two sets of rear gears, allowing much better top-end speed while maintaining the quick acceleration of the deeper gears.

All GM non-overdrive (manual or automatic) transmissions eventually produce a 1:1 gear ratio. Some overdrive transmissions have two overdrives, such as the Tremec T-56, allowing even larger gears to be used.

Tires

Tire size is another important factor in gear selection. Tire sizes vary greatly from vehicle to vehicle, so it is difficult to determine which is best. The formula for comparing tire sizes is as follows:

Effective Gear Ratio = new tire diameter ÷ old tire diameter x old gear ratio

For example, if you have a car with a 3.73:1 gear set and 28-inch-tall tires, and you want to increase the tire size to 30 inches, the final drive is 3.16:1 (28 ÷ 33 x 3.73), which means less acceleration but higher top-end speed.

You can also use this formula to compare the effects of gears and tires for many applications. For instance, a vehicle with 4.11 gears and 28-inch tires, moving to 30-inch tires, has the opposite effect: a 4.40:1 effective ratio (30 ÷ 28 x 4.11). This means that the car accelerates more quickly, but with less top-end speed.

And you can use this formula to extrapolate the effectiveness of your gearing change. With 30-inch tires, the effective ratio of a 4.11 gear is the same as a 28-inch tire with 3.73 gears. This makes 4.11 gears with an overdrive transmission and 30-inch tires very effective for street use, but requires shorter tires for drag racing.

Diving deeper into the realm of gearing calculations, the following formula helps you make your gearing decision:

$$MPH = (RPM \times \text{tire circumference in feet}) \div (\text{rear gear ratio} \times \text{transmission gear ratio} \times 88)$$

Where:
MPH = desired operating speed
88 = mathematical constant

For this calculation, the formula will be shortened for a 1:1 transmission gear.

This is helpful for calculating the actual (or theoretical) results of a gear or tire change at a specific RPM or speed. For instance, a vehicle with 30-inch tires, 4.11 gears spinning at 4,000 rpm travels at 87 mph [(4,000 x 7.85) ÷ (4.11 x 88)].

You can look up the tire circumference for your specific brand and size or calculate it by using the following formula:

$$\text{Tire Circumference} = \text{overall tire diameter} \times 3.14 \div 12$$

Where:
3.14 = mathematical constant (pi)
12 = number of inches in a foot

For example, the circumference of a 30-inch tire is 7.85 feet (30 x 3.14 ÷ 12).

If you change to 3.73 gears, the vehicle travels at 96 mph [(31,400) ÷ (3.73 x 88)].

You can achieve a big difference in overall speed by simply changing to a lower numerical gear. If math is not your strong suit, many calculators are available online to calculate the gear ratios. Some calculators show you the top speed for every gear.

Ring Gears and Carrier

As you know, the pinion gear becomes smaller as the ratio increases numerically, so the ring gear mounting depth must be considered. The pinion position is not variable from side to side; it is in a fixed position inside the housing. The ring gear carrier has a small amount of adjustment from side to side. As the pinion gear changes in size, the position of the ring gear to the pinion must change.

GM differential carriers accommodate a small range of ratios so the gear mesh is maintained. The result is three carrier sizes. All GM 10- and 12-bolt variants use similar ranges.

Factory Carriers

The factory carriers for the 12-bolt passenger car are available in the following sizes:
2-Series: Gear ratio is 2.56 to 2.73:1. Bearing shoulder-to-ring gear surface is 0.590 inch. This is the smallest of the stock GM carriers. It is weak and not suitable for performance applications.
3-Series: Gear ratio is 3.07 to 3.73:1. Bearing shoulder-to-ring gear surface is 1.12 inches.
4-Series: Gear ratio is 4.10 to 4.88:1. Bearing shoulder-to-ring gear surface is 1.325 inches.

Aftermarket Carriers

Although most aftermarket carriers provide their own details, they tend to follow these guidelines:
2-Series: Gear ratio 2.73:1 and lower.
3-Series: Gear ratio 3.08:1 to 3.90:1.
4-Series: Gear ratio 4.10:1 and higher.

For non-performance applications, a spacer can be used to step up a smaller carrier to the next size, such as a 2-Series for a 3-Series gear. These *are not* for performance applications,

as there is a lot more stress put on the longer bolts than they can handle; they eventually fail in spectacular fashion.

Ring Gear Bolts

General Motors used bolts with different sizes and thread pitches for the ring gear. For 10- and 12-bolt units, the ring gear bolts are 7/16-inch fine-thread bolts with a large 9/16-inch hex-head cap. Left-hand-thread bolts in the ring gear were used with some 10-bolt units. "L" is marked on some but not all of these bolts.

The point is to be careful and check the bolts before taking them off with an impact wrench. Many front-wheel-drive carriers also use left-hand threads.

Ring gear bolts are secured with thread locker, which prevents them from loosening because of the many heat cycles experienced throughout their life. If you leave the thread locker off during your installation, you will likely find out the hard way.

Bearing Installation

Before installing new gears into the housing, you need to follow a few

A damaged pinion shaft wreaks havoc on the rest of the internals as well. Oil starvation causes this kind of damage. The bearings overheat and seize onto the pinion.

procedures. All ring-and-pinion gears are forged. In the forging process, they are formed through a series of operations that take a piece of solid billet steel, heat it to red hot, and slam it into a press to form the basic shape. The next press forms the general ring or pinion shape, and then the actual teeth are cut into the gears during the machining phase.

After the machine work is completed, the gears are heat treated and quenched in oil to induce a hard outer surface that is generally .050 inch deep, while maintaining a softer inner core that allows the gears to flex enough so that they don't break under extreme conditions. This is much like a sword wherein the outer surface is very hard so that the steel can hold an edge, but the inner core of the metal is soft enough to allow it to flex so it doesn't shatter on impact with an unyielding surface.

Special Tool

1 Remove Pinion Bearing

A bearing separator, such as this, can be used in a hydraulic press to remove the pinion bearing. If you do not own or have access to a hydraulic press, you need to have a shop remove the bearing. The separator tool simply supports the bearing. You want to keep the original bearing intact for setting up the new gears if at all possible, otherwise you have to ruin a perfectly good bearing for the set-up phase. It will be replaced later, but you need one to set the pinion depth.

3 Inspect Pinion Shim

4 Inspect Pinion Shim *(CONTINUED)*

2 Inspect Bearing

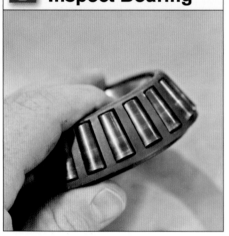

Although this inner bearing did not seize, the bluing on the bearing rollers means it was close to failing. If it had failed, it could have cracked the rear-end housing.

Under the bearing is the factory shim. You can try to reuse it, but you will likely have to add shims or replace it with a thinner shim to get the new gears to mesh correctly.

Several new shims are included with a rebuild kit. A shim sets the pinion depth; it is not a wear part. Shims come in varying thicknesses, but it is always a good idea to start with the original one and go from there.

5 Install Inner Bearing

The inner bearing is a press-on part, so you need a slip-fit bearing as a stand-in for setting up the gears. Modify the original bearing (it will be replaced) for fitment over the pinion gear. Use a carbide burr or sanding roll with a die grinder to open it up just enough so that it slips on and off the new pinion gear easily.

6 Install Inner Bearing (CONTINUED)

Once the bearing has been modified, slip the shims over the pinion shaft and place the bearing on top of them.

Professional Mechanic Tip [PRO TIP]

7 Install Pinion Gear in Housing

[PRO TIP] You need to perform an initial fitment so you need to mock up the differential in the housing before you perform the final assembly. Place the pinion in the case and prelube the bearings so that they don't stick.

8 Install Solid Spacer

All GM 10- and 12-bolt axles use crush sleeves. Do not install the crush sleeves yet; you are simply trying to figure out the initial settings. The crush sleeves should only be used for final assembly because once they crush, they can't be reused.

9 Install Solid Spacer (CONTINUED)

A solid spacer is an alternative to a crush sleeve. It does not crush; rather, it uses shims to set the pinion pre-load. It is re-useable and not difficult to set up.

10 Install Solid Spacer (CONTINUED)

Push the crush sleeve in from the front of the case. If you are setting up a solid spacer sleeve, wait until the pinion depth is set to do so.

11 Install New Pinion Bearing

Install the new front bearing into the case. On new pinions, the bearing is likely very tight. You may need to use the yoke and pinion nut to pull the pinion into the bearing.

Ring and Pinion Machining

You have a choice between two- and five-cut machining processes for ring and pinion gears. The backlash must be set differently for each cut style. The mesh patterns vary as well. The two-cut gears are the same height from heel to toe. The wear pattern is biased or angled on the edges (in parallel) in a square form. Five-cut gears are machined with a shorter toe and taller heel. The wear pattern shows up as a wide rectangle or oval shape.

Be sure to follow the correct backlash spec for the type of gears you have. GM 12-bolt units are all five-cut, but both styles are available for 8.5- and 8.6-inch 10-bolts. Two-cut gears require a tighter backlash, between .0030 and .0060 inch, in which five-cut gears are much wider with a sweet spot generally between .0060 and .010 inch.

Once completed, each gear set is lapped together to make them a matched set forever. This process is essentially a polishing method that ensures the gears mesh together.

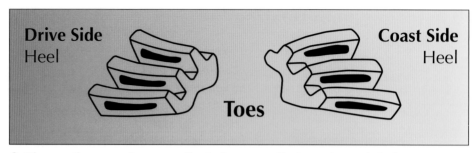

Setting up the gears is a complicated process that requires a lot of trial-and-error test fitting. One of the tests is a grease mark that shows the mesh pattern. This is the proper centering as shown on the ring gear.

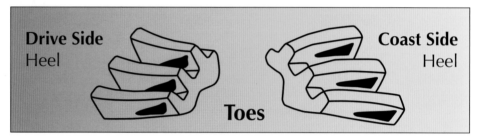

When the pinion is too close to the ring gear, you get a pattern like this.

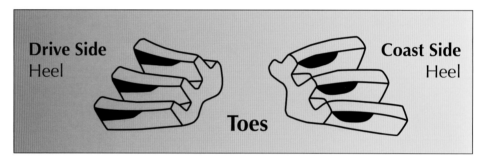

If the pinion gear is too far away from the ring gear, the result looks like this.

Here is what a proper mesh pattern looks like. See Chapter 7 for more details.

1 Press Bearing and Shims onto Pinion Gear

Once the pinion depth is set, press the new bearing and correct shims onto the pinion gear. This requires a hydraulic press; you can't do it any other way.

2 Prep Ring Gear for Installation

Inspect the ring gear for burrs before installing it on the carrier. Using a flat file removes any burrs without gouging into the gear.

Each gear is installed into a special machine that puts a slight load onto the gears and spins them while they bathe in silicon-carbide abrasive media. This removes any imperfections in the gear teeth as well as corrects any issues with spiral angle, spacing, or eccentricity. Once lapped, the gears are forever a pair and should never be mixed with others gears.

Torque Fasteners

3 Install Carrier on Ring Gear

To attach the carrier to the ring gear you thread in two bolts at opposite ends of the carrier. Then use thread lube and thread the rest of the bolts into the ring gear. Using a star torqueing pattern, torque all the bolts to the ring gear. Remember that ring gear torque specs are different for various differentials. In addition, you must follow your hardware supplier's torque specs. Most 10-bolts are torqued to 65 ft-lbs while 12-bolts (car and truck) are typically 55 ft-lbs.

This manufacturing process creates a sturdy component that will last for years of service, but the occasional issue may arise, such as burrs on the threads of the mating surfaces.

Inspect the gears as soon as you open the box. Look for anything that may snag on the carrier or bearings. If you find a burr, it can be removed carefully with a file.

Speedometers

When the gear ratio is changed, the speedometer gearing is altered. When you change gear ratios on vehicles with electronic speedometers, you need to reprogram the computer or follow a calibration process for aftermarket speedos. With mechanical speedometers, you must calculate the exact transmission ratio for your gears and tires.

Most GM transmissions have readily available gear sets to match

your application. The driven gear is the gear installed into the removable housing; the drive gear is the gear inside the transmission on the output shaft. Sometimes this gear must be changed to accommodate your combination, but this is not common.

The cable drive for the speedometer is located on the driver's side of the transmission; a clamp and a bolt usually retain it or it may be threaded into the housing itself. Remove the threaded cable

and then remove the speedo drive. Most GM transmissions use a nylon gear on the end that is color coded to match a specific ratio. Typical GM driven-gear housings come in two driven-gear groups: those with 34 to 39 teeth and those with 40 to 45 teeth.

Find Speedometer Gear

To determine what speedometer gear you need, start by measuring the tire diameter with the tire on the ground. Measure from the ground to

GM Drive Gears

TurboHydramatic 350 and Super T-10, T5 (with TH350 housing) Manual		TurboHydramatic 400		2004R	
Cable End Color	Tooth Count	Cable End Color	Tooth Count	Cable End Color	Tooth Count
Pink	7	Red	7	Green	10
Black	8	Black	8	Orange	11
Green	9	Brown or Gray	9	Red	12
Red or Purple	10	Orange	16	White	13
Red	17	Red	17	**700R-4 and 4L60E**	
Blue	18	Yellow or Blue	18	Cable End Color	Tooth Count
Yellow	19	Yellow or White	19	Gray	15
Brown	20	Green	20	Red	17
		Black	21	Blue	18
				Yellow	19 ■

the centerline of the axle and multiply by two.

For a more accurate result, take into account the flattening of the tire's contact patch. You could use the factory tire spec if you don't have the actual tires available to measure.

Plug those measurements into the following formulas:

Number of Driven Teeth =
(number of drive teeth x gear ratio x tire revolutions per mile) ÷ 1,001

Where:
1,001 = mathematical constant

Tire Revolutions per Mile =
20,168 ÷ tire diameter

Where:
20,168 = mathematical constant

For example, a GM 700R4 transmission with a 15-tooth drive gear, 3.73 gears, and 28-inch tires does 720.28 tire revolutions per mile (20,168 ÷ 28) and has 40 driven teeth (15 x 3.73 x 720.28 ÷ 1,001).

GM 700R4 and 4L60E Transmissions

With 15-Tooth Drive Gear			With 17-Tooth Drive Gear		
Axle Ratio (:1)	Tire Height (inches)	Driven-Gear Tooth Count	Axle Ratio (:1)	Tire Height (inches)	Driven-Gear Tooth Count
4.56	33	42	3.73	28	45
4.56	35	39	3.73	29	44
4.10	26	45 (does work, but reads about 3 mph fast at 50 mph)	3.42	26	45
4.10	27	45	3.42	26½	44
4.10	28	44	3.42	27	43
4.10	29	43	3.42	28	42
4.10	30	41			
4.10	31	40	**With 18-Tooth Drive Gear**		
4.10	33	38	Axle Ratio (:1)	Tire Height (inches)	Driven-Gear Tooth Count
4.10	35	35	3.23	26	45
3.73	26	43	3.23	26½	44
3.73	27	42	3.23	27	43
3.73	27½	41	3.23	28	42 ■
3.73	28	40			
3.73	29	39			
3.73	30	38			
3.73	31	36			

Speedometer Driven Gears

ach speedometer driven gear corresponds to a different color and tooth count for each transmission it fits. Here are the GM color codes for the driven gears. Chevy housings use a 1-inch driven-gear housing, while the Buick, Oldsmobile, and Pontiac units use a 2.078-inch driven-gear housing in aluminum or plastic in the standard GM gear ranges.

If there is not a gear that exactly matches your application, the standard practice is to use the smaller of the closest two gears. This makes your speedometer run slightly faster than the "correct" gear. GM's spec is for the speedometer to read between 60 and 63 mph when the speedometer shows "60." This is the factory variance. It is considered better to be actually slower than your speedometer rather than appearing to be traveling faster. ∎

Tremec T-5, Super T10, and Muncie 4-Speed

Cable End Color	Tooth Count	Cable End Color	Tooth Count
brown	18	blue	38
natural	19	brown	39
blue	20	black	40
red	21	yellow	41
gray	22	green	42
light green	34	purple	43
orange/pink	35	dark gray	44
white	36	light blue	45
red	37		

2004R Transmissions

Cable End Color	Tooth Count	Cable End Color	Tooth Count
brown	26	green	29
black	27	blue	30
yellow	28	white	31

TH400 Transmissions

Cable End Color	Tooth Count	Cable End Color	Tooth Count
truck	16	red	37
truck	17	blue	38
truck code H	18	brown	39
truck code J	19	black	40
truck code K	20	yellow	41
truck code L	21	green	42
truck code M	22	purple	43
light green	34	dark gray	44
pink	35	light blue	45
white	36		

700R4 and 4L60E Transmissions

Cable End Color	Tooth Count	Cable End Color	Tooth Count
brown (truck)	18	red	37
dark aqua (truck)	19	blue	38
silver (truck)	20	brown	39
red/chartreuse (truck)	21	black	40
gold (truck)	22	yellow	41
maroon (truck)	23	green	42
dark blue (truck)	24	purple	43
light green	34	dark gray	44
orange/pink	35	light blue	45
white	36		

AXLES

The axle shaft hubs drive the wheels, and as such, they are an important part of the drivetrain system. Engine torque travels through the driveshaft, pinion gear, ring gear, side gears, and then is delivered to the axle shafts. Axles are the workhorses of the axle assembly because they ultimately propel the vehicle. If the axles break, the car loses its drive, and it might not even roll.

Torque Load

Axles are simple components that have a long shaft with splines on one end and a flange on the other, which is drilled for the wheels. The axles see the most brutal application of torque for the entire vehicle. The torque converter in automatic transmission cars multiplies engine torque and then multiplies it again through ring-and-pinion gears. Thousands of foot-pounds hit the axles every time you stomp on the gas pedal. Dump the clutch for a manual, and the shock is even bigger. Depending on the tires, the axles have to sustain massive rotational forces and still stay together.

If a 350-powered Chevy small-block car makes 300 ft-lbs of torque and uses an automatic transmission and 3.55:1 gears, each axle receives more than 2,300 ft-lbs of torque. If the tires spin from heavy acceleration, this number decreases. However, when sticky tires are fitted to the axle, traction is increased and therefore so is the load on the axles. Too much torque load for the axles results in a rotational fracture and axle failure.

Other loads are at work on the axles as well. Both GM 10- and 12-bolt differentials are a semi-float design, which means that the axles carry the weight of the vehicle on one bearing at the end of the axle shaft. The axle bearings, or wheel bearings, must support the entire weight of the vehicle. Therefore, the bearings need to be in good condition and the axle surface they ride on needs to be perfectly round and smooth.

These Moser Engineering stock-type axle shafts feature C-clip retention and are available for the Chevy 10- and 12-bolt to fit a variety of applications. (Photo Courtesy Moser Engineering)

Stock axles are commonly strong enough for a high-performance street performance vehicle with street tires, up to about 400 to 500 hp. Axles are the hardest-working component inside the housing, translating thousands of pounds of torque into forward motion and supporting the weight of the vehicle through rough street conditions.

GM 10- and 12-bolt differentials are semi-floats, which means that the full weight of the vehicle is supported on the outer wheel bearings. The wheel bearing end on the housing holds two components: the bearing and the seal.

When the bearings fail, the result is damage. You can clearly see pitting, discoloration, and grooving from worn bearings. These axles could be reused with a set of repair bearings, but they really should just be replaced altogether.

A repair bearing provides a solution to typical bearing damage. The bearing is moved about 1 inch from the inside to the outside of the axle where it should ride on fresh steel. The seal is integrated into the bearing housing, making it a one-piece component.

The bearing has an outer seal and an O-ring seal on the inside.

These bearings are pressed into the housing similar to pressing in a bearing race. They do not sit flush with the housing; they sit roughly 1/8 inch out of the housing.

A typical street axle must cope with enormous side loads. Every corner means that the one axle is pushing in on the wheel bearings and cross-shaft pin in the differential, while the opposing axle is pulling on the C-clip. Most high-performance cars run sticky tires, so these forces dramatically increase, putting several hundred tons of force on the bearings and the 1/4-inch-thick area that retains the C-clip.

Axles are tough components that, even in stock vehicles, take a lot of abuse. And if you add more power and harder driving conditions, they simply must be capable of taking a beating. In the final analysis, the axles used in your housing are just as important as the gears and differential.

Spline Design

Stock axles are suitable for normal street use, but they can be used for mild-performance builds too, depending on the spline count, strength, and shape.

Here, a 28-spline axle (left) is compared to a 33-spline axle (right). The difference is nearly 1/4-inch diameter, which is an increase of approximately 33 percent. Note that the shape of the splines are the same.

Axle Shaft Strength

Spline Count	Diameter (inches)	Strength Increase (percent)
28	1.205	Baseline
31	1.330	+/− 35
33	1.413	+/− 60
35	1.500	+/− 77
40	1.710	+/− 198

Spline Count

The spline count is the number of splines on the axle shaft. Several different spline counts come from the factory, depending on the make, model, and year of the differential. For custom-built rears, you have your choice, but how do you choose the appropriate spline count for your application?

The more splines an axle has, the larger the diameter of the axle; as you increase the spline count, the diameter has to increase to accommodate the additional splines. Each spline is the same size whether the axle has 28 or 35 splines. A typical GM 8.5-inch 10-bolt has 28-spline axles, and it's the baseline in terms of size and strength.

Most 8.5-inch 10-bolts installed in trucks received 30-spline axles. The actual outside diameter (OD) of a 28-spline axle is 1.205 inches while the 30-spline axle is larger at 1.310 inches. Therefore, the 30-spline axle is 35 percent stronger than the 28-spline.

Anytime you increase the spline count, the differential carrier must be upgraded to match the axle diameter of the particular shafts. So arbitrarily upgrading to a larger count costs you money that may be better spent elsewhere. When it comes to

Axles are available in different sizes and spline counts. The more splines on the shaft, the larger the diameter of the axle. Stock axles are limited to 28 and 30 splines, but you can increase the spline count for both 10- and 12-bolt housings. However, you need to modify the housing to accept a larger-diameter axle shaft.

spline count, bigger is better, but it isn't always necessary. Manufacturers offer guidance for a particular vehicle, engine, transmission, and other factors, so you can select the correct axle shafts for your combination.

When it comes to spline count, there isn't a magic formula or number for determining axle strength because other variables are at play, such as tires, transmission, intended use, etc. For example, a 700-hp full-race drag car with slicks and a transmission brake would put more stress on the driveline than a street-tired foot-brake car with 1,000 hp.

Spline Strength

The way the splines are created makes a difference too. Four factors determine spline strength: count, pressure angle, major diameter, and minor diameter.

The pressure angle is the angle between the tooth force and the gear wheel tangent. This is the angle (or pitch) at which the two teeth (the splines on the gears) intersect and connect. Most axles are either 45 or 30 degrees.

The major diameter is the OD of the spline circle at the top land. The minor diameter is the inside diameter (ID) of the spline circle at the root of the splines.

All modern axles are designed with a 24-degree angle for the splines. Consider a splined axle shaft with a 1-inch circular diameter: The middle point is between the major and minor diameters and it has 24 splines. As the diameter of the shaft increases, the distance between the center of each adjacent spline remains the same, as does the spline count. For example, a 35-spline axle has a major diameter of 1.50 inches; a 30-spline axle is 1.31 inches in diameter.

Spline Shape

Another key characteristic of the spline is its shape. All OEM axles and differentials use involute splines. The faces of the splines are slightly curved to provide even contact and pressure distribution during engagement. Rolling the splines into the axles does several things. First, the involute design uses a curved sur-

The splines are said to be "involute." This means that the faces of the teeth are slightly curved. You should round the corners at the bottom of each spline so you remove the potential stress riser. It is a key indication for determining how the splines were created. Only rolled or hobbed splines have this shape.

face, and a standard flycut machine can cut this surface. Second, the metallurgy of a rolled spline determines its strength and elasticity, which is an important factor.

Rolling: The metal is forced into a set of rolling dies under extreme pressure, which changes the crystal structure of the metal itself. The molecules of the metal align, becoming denser, and thus the metal is stronger. After the splines are rolled, the axle is then heat-treated.

Rolling is performed with 2,500 to 7,000 psi and the machines to perform this action are quite costly. Therefore, most custom axles are made with a different manufacturing method.

Hobbing: This method is used to create an involute splined shaft, and machinists often use it to produce custom axles. A spline hob is a specialized machine that cuts all the splines at once. The hobbing process yields an accurate involute spline,

When measuring axles for replacement, make sure that you follow the specs provided by the manufacturer. The top axle is a factory piece with rolled splines; the spline stops at the base. The bottom axle has hobbed splines; the splines tape off as they were cut.

Axle blanks are forged for strength and then machined to match the profile necessary.

The final spline looks similar to rolled splines and is as strong. The axle is now ready for heat treating.

A metal lathe with a special spline tool is used to cut splines. Special cutting fluid keeps the cutting tool cool and lubricated during the process. (Photo Courtesy Strange Engineering)

and when done before the shaft is hardened is just about as accurate as a rolled spline.

Flycutting: Most machine shops can flycut axle shafts. Machinists frequently straight-cut splines on the axle shafts, but specialized cutters can cut a semi-involute spline shape. The key to a properly flycut spline is keeping the depth above the hardening line, or having the axle re-hardened once cut.

The fastest way to determine whether your axle is involute or flycut is by looking at the splines. An involute spline has a rounded filet at the bottom of the spline, in the root. Flycut splines show a boxed corner angle.

Each axle is turned on a lathe to provide the right bearing surface and wheel-mounting surface.

There are a couple of potential strength issues with cut splines. Cutting means ripping away metal. Regardless of how fine the cut is, it still rips the material apart. This results in potential stress risers that could cause a failure. The other potential problem is that splines have to mesh with an involute spline in the differential side gears.

Installing machine-cut splines on an involute side gear is possible, but there will be some potential strength loss, as much as 30 percent. The issue

Factory Axle Specs				
Housing	Spline Count	Pressure Angle (degrees)	Major Diameter (inches)	Minor Diameter (inches)
7.5-inch 10-bolt	26	45	1.1250	1.0321
8.2- and 8.5-inch 10-bolt (1965–1981)	28	45	1.2083	1.1154
Buick and Pontiac 8.2-inch 10-bolt (1964–1970)	28	45	1.2083	1.1154
12-bolt Passenger Car and Truck	30	45	1.2917	1.2083

is that the angles won't be an exact match, which puts undue stress on the splines. Spline failure is not that common, but it does happen, and it is usually a result of straight-cut splines.

Stock versus Aftermarket Axles

Only a few stock axles are offered for the Chevy 10- and 12-bolt. The only stock axles available for the GM truck 10- and 12-bolt units are

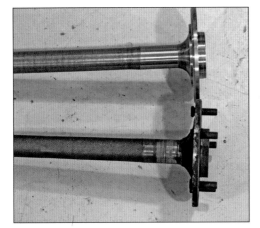

28-spline, and this axle shaft fits only the 8.5-inch 10-bolt. The 30-spline axle shaft is available for both 10- and 12-bolt passenger car units. The 7.5- and 8.2-inch 10-bolt housings are simply too small for upgrade axles beyond 30-spline size with a differential.

Aftermarket axles provide some upgrade potential, but size is not one of them. The truck 12-bolt had two factory axle sizes. The early trucks use a 12-spline axle, which does not provide enough strength so it is not

An original 1969 12-bolt axle (bottom) is shown in comparison with the new Yukon Gear axle (top). They are the same except that the upper axle has more defined features. It's something you would expect from a performance part, rather than a mass-produced factory piece.

used for high-performance applications. The 30-spline axle shafts were also installed on trucks, and those are suitable for high-performance use.

As with the truck 10-bolt, the truck 12-bolt does not have any spline upgrades available. That said, 30-spline axles are not weak. The 8.5-inch 10-bolt is capable of handling large amounts of torque. For example, a Buick Grand National 3.8 turbo has the reputation for hanging the front wheels well past the 60-foot mark on the dragstrip with the stock 8.5 10-bolt axle assembly.

The aftermarket offers the passenger car 12-bolt with larger 33- and 35-spline axles. However, you need to install a larger aftermarket housing or center section to accommodate those larger-diameter axle shafts. The 33-spline axles measure 1.41 inches, with a whopping 1.50-inch diameter in the 35-spline units.

Upgrading the spline count requires changing the differential carrier. The 33-spline option requires an Eaton Truetrac gear-driven LSD. Switching to the massive 35-spline carrier means upgrading to a Detroit Locker.

One other option for all three differentials is available: a spool. By switching to a spool from a differential, you have more room for larger-diameter axles. Moreover, 33- and 35-spline axles are available for the 8.5-inch 10-bolt and the truck 12-bolt. Keep in mind, however, that a spool *is not* street friendly. In fact, they can be dangerous on the street.

Aftermarket Upgrades

Every car has specific needs in terms of axles, such as vehicle weight, power potential, tire size and

Bolt-in axles for the Buick and Olds 8.2 and 8.5 10-bolts feature a press-on bearing, shims, and mounting flange. If you convert your housing to bolt-in axles, it is the same for your new axles.

type; even the elapsed time for drag racers factors in to the final determination. Anytime you are unsure of your application's specific needs, give one of the manufacturers a call. Their tech department will gladly answer any questions you have to ensure you get the right axles for your application.

Stock Chevy 10- and 12-bolt axle assemblies support up to 400 hp on street tires, with less on drag radials and even less on slicks. If your car is producing more than 400 hp and/or fitted with drag radials or slicks, stock axles cannot support this so they will most likely fail. Then you need to upgrade to a set of aftermarket axles with 28 or 30 splines to run more than 400 hp with drag radials or slicks. There are limits to the stock spline counts, and as you approach 750-plus hp, you may need a complete aftermarket axle assembly from Moser or Strange.

This means that you can bolt a set of drag slicks to an otherwise stock 8.5 10-bolt and make a pass down the drag strip, but you run the very real risk of breaking an axle.

Material

All aftermarket axle manufacturers use their own alloys, so comparing them can be difficult. However, comparing those to OEM axles is simple enough. Most OEM axles are made from either 1039 steel (for flange-mount bearings) or 1050 steel (for C-clips). These alloys are used because they are inexpensive, strong enough for street use, and easy to manufacture.

Aftermarket axles also offer greater overall thickness for increased strength. Factory axles are typically necked-down several inches from the end while after-

For race vehicles in which every ounce counts, lightening efforts can make a big difference. These Strange axles have lightening holes in the wheel flange. (Photo Courtesy Strange Engineering)

market axles remain at their full diameter right up to the start of the splined area. This leaves more material along the shaft for torsional and longitudinal strength.

Aftermarket axles use a wider range of alloys, depending on the manufacturer's design. Strange Engineering uses Hy-Tuf alloy, which is proprietary steel. This low-carbon, high-manganese, high-nickel, and high-molybdenum steel was originally developed for landing gear in military aircraft, making it a logical choice for race axles.

Moser Engineering uses 1541H alloy steel for all of their axles, including stock replacement axles. The stronger the alloy, the stronger the axle. Most of the leading brands use 1541H alloy for 10- and 12-bolt axles.

Moser takes lightening a bit further with drastically machined wheel flanges. (Photo Courtesy Moser Engineering)

Gun drilling can reduce axle weight by up to 20 percent, but it comes with a cost. Gun-drilled axles are not as strong in terms of longitudinal force, so they can't take the bending forces experienced on the street. (Photo Courtesy Strange Engineering)

This axle end shows how much material can be removed by gun drilling. (Photo Courtesy Strange Engineering)

Shaft Retention

The method of axle shaft retention is an important consideration. C-clips are by far the most common axle retainers, but they are also not legal for drag racing below 10.99 ET. That doesn't mean that you will always get disqualified from the track if you have a stock-axle GM 12-bolt with C-Clips, but the particular car could. It all depends on the application.

C-clips are located past the splines on the axle in the center of the differential, so there is nothing keeping the axle inside the tube at the end of the housing. When the axle shaft breaks, the wheel can come out of the car, creating a potentially dangerous situation for everyone around it and being particularly destructive for the car. For a 10.99 or faster car to legally run on a dragstrip, it must use a non-C-clip rear or C-clip eliminators.

Eliminators retain the axle at the end of the axle tube flange, so if the axle breaks, the wheel does not come out of the car. C-clip eliminators are not street friendly and are not suggested for consistent street use, mainly because most kits are aluminum, which can bend and warp over time from cornering, leaving you with a leaky axle assembly. These kits are available for the 10- and 12-bolt housings from Moser Engineering, Yukon Gear, and Strange Engineering. (See Chapter 2 for more detail on C-clip eliminators.)

The other most common axle shaft retention method is a flange style. The Ford 9-inch and a few differentials use flange axle tubes. With the flange retainer, four bolts and a plate keep the outer wheel bearing in the housing, and this retains the axle shaft inside the tube. Similar to a C-clip eliminator, when an axle breaks on a flange style tube, the flange holds the broken axle shaft and the wheel continues to spin on the axle.

This is one of the greatest assets of the Ford 9-inch. Certain GM axle assemblies use this design as well, specifically the Buick, Oldsmobile, and the occasional Pontiac 8.5-inch 10-bolt in A-Body cars. These axles are hard to find, and they can only be distinguished by taking them apart. Not all Buick and Pontiac A-Bodies used the non-C-clip rear; finding one is really just a big crapshoot.

Heat Treating

Heat treating is an important process that increases the strength of the axle shafts. Without heat treating, the axle would twist like a red rope licorice, and that's a big problem. Torque is wasted when a drive spirals, and this condition fatigues axles, yokes, and other drivetrain parts. So, failures can occur.

Induction Hardening

Axles must be hardened in order to live under the stress of heavy torque. How deep the axle is hardened is key to its function. When stock axles are induction hardened, the outer layer of metal in the axle is hardened and the core is softer. This is achieved by heating up the axle quickly, typically by running it through a heating coil then quenching it in oil or water. The outside of the metal heats up much faster than the inside. When it is quenched, only the outer shell of the metal is hardened.

Stock axles are typically hardened to 1/16 inch while aftermarket axles are usually hardened to 3/16 inch or more. Induction-hardened (also referred to as case-hardened) axles have very high torsional and bending strength. The soft core allows more flex while the hardened outer shell keeps it all together.

Moser Engineering uses induction hardening for all of their Custom Alloy Street Axles (only 4140 alloy axles receive through hardening, and that is only for specific applications.) Moser performs all heat treating in its own facility using the induction process. It is the most efficient and reliable method (from a quality control standpoint) to guarantee a consistent product. The depth of the heat treat varies depending on the diameter of the shaft and the spline count.

Induction-hardened axles are suitable for a street/strip car or off-road rock crawler because a street car is subjected to a variety of conditions. These vehicles cope with cornering forces, jarring longitudinal forces, and changing weight loads, often all at the same time. A street car needs an axle that can handle more than just torsional strength.

Through Hardening

Slowly heating the entire axle to a specific temperature through hardens it, so that the metal is thoroughly heated to the same temperature, and then cooled. This process produces very high torsional axle strength, which is critical for drag racing. Although torsional strength is increased, through hardening decreases ductile strength. Ductile strength is the metal's ability to spring back from bending.

Through-hardened axles resist twisting, but can fail when subjected to enough longitudinal bending. Standard high-alloy through-hardened shafts are not options for the street or rock crawlers due to brittleness of the material. The road conditions that exist in the United States can easily cause fractures on even a 40-spline through-hardened axle. Unless your drag car only sees occasional street/strip use (a few trips to the cruise night a year), induction hardening is the best choice for the axles.

Weight Saving

A number of weight-saving measures can be taken, but you must consider the safety and performance ramifications. An easy and common way to increase dragstrip ETs is to shave a little weight off the axle. But you must not compromise the structural integrity of the axle assembly.

Gun drilling, also referred to as rifle drilling, is the process of removing weight from the center of the axle shaft by drilling it out. This can reduce the weight of an axle by as much as 17 to 26 percent. Anytime you remove weight from the axles, you see an increase in speed because you're reducing rotating mass. However, the drawback is reduced strength of the axle. And this is a particular concern for a street car

because the potholes, corners, and bumps it encounters add to the stress on the axle.

As a result, I do not recommend gun-drilled axles for a car that sees regular street use because one significant impact, such as hitting a bad spot in the pavement or pothole, increases the possibility of breakage. An airplane's fuselage can flex ever so slightly and not fracture, and you want some of the same characteristics for a street axle. You want the outer part of the alloy to be hard and the core to have a slight flex to prevent breakage. There are weight limits for drilled axles, so check with your manufacturer to ensure that your decision is a safe one.

You can also remove weight from the wheel hub to lighten the axle. Most aftermarket axle manufacturers offer lightened axles. But you don't have to buy custom axles for every car and application.

Lightweight cars, such as street rods and fiberglass-bodied dragsters, don't put as much stress on the axles as a full-size 1970 Buick GS, which tips the scales at 4,000 pounds.

Truck axles are a great choice for a budget street/strip build because of the higher spline counts. With thicker flanges, this means that they can handle more torsional and longitudinal stress, especially in a light car, such as a T-bucket dragster. Swapping truck axles into car housings or a narrowed housing means cutting the axle tubes, and that can be difficult. Most aftermarket axle manufacturers offer custom cutting and splining services, but that means shipping them back and forth, which, of course, takes additional time and money.

Another option is to find a local machine shop that can cut splines. If you can find one, your options greatly increase. You need to order a set of uncut axles with no bolt pattern or splines and have your local guy do the finish work. That way, you get what you want to fit your housing. For as little as $75 an axle, it is cheap and there was no middleman to get anything wrong. Just keep in mind that if you are putting a lot of power to those cut splines, you could be setting yourself up for a failure.

Project: Replacing Wheel Studs

Wheel studs fail and it's not uncommon when you are running a muscle car. Let me paint a picture for you: Sweat is beading up on your forehead, the midday sun is blistering the skin on the back of your neck, and a blast of 80-mph wind just about knocks you over from the semi-truck screaming down the highway.

You had a blow out, and now you are stuck on the shoulder of a busy highway swapping tires. Each lug nut comes off, the new tire goes on, and then you start

cranking down on the lugs, making sure that they are tight; after all, the only thing worse than a blow out is losing the entire wheel. Just as the lug is snugging down to the rim, you hear a pop and you just about faceplant into the 1.5-million-degree asphalt. Yeah, you really did it this time; you busted a wheel stud.

Don't stress too much; it happens. Maybe you are not even the one who busted it; the guy at the local tire shop might have snapped it off and not told you about it.

(It happens more often that you think.) But the situation is the same. The results are the same; a busted wheel stud and you have to drive around with one less lug nut on your car. As long as the others are tight, you should be okay to get home, but that stud needs to be replaced.

Fortunately, there is an easy way to fix a busted wheel stud without taking half of your vehicle's suspension apart.

If you do not have an impact wrench, you can use a socket wrench,

Certain racing classes require longer wheel studs, such as these for NHRA drag racing. All new axles require the installation of new studs.

Studs are easily removed from old axles. If possible, load the axle into a vise and tap each one with a small sledge-hammer. It usually does not take much effort to remove the studs from the axle; just watch your fingers. Never reinstall old studs into new or used axles.

A missing stud on an axle or rotor hub on the car can throw you off. Don't worry; there is an easy fix.

For long axles, special open-end lug nuts such as this are required. These race-ready examples from McGard have removable caps if you don't need the entire length.

Installing the new studs can be done several ways, depending on the tools you have available and whether the axle is in the housing. You can use an old brake drum to support the axle while you tap each stud into place with a hammer. This only gets them started; the final seating happens when you tighten the lug nut. A press is the best method if you have one available.

Insert the new stud from the back of the flange, then install the brake rotor over the flange.

Stack a few washers onto the stud, along with a lug nut. If you don't have a brake rotor, you can just use more washers.

but you will need a way to lock the axle hub from spinning. The following process works on front hubs and rear axles. The entire process typically takes about 20 minutes to complete.

Remove the lug nut and washers. Check the fitment of the stud. The head of the stud should be flush with the backside of the axle hub.

Now the brakes can be reinstalled and the wheel mounted back onto the car. Install the lug nuts in a star pattern, tightening each one hand-tight to secure the wheel.

Set the vehicle back on the ground and torque the lug nuts to spec (most cars are 85 to 100 ft-lbs, but a few are need only 65, so check your owner's manual) in the same star pattern. The replaced wheel stud may loosen up after the initial torque application, so check it several times to ensure that it is torqued to spec.

While holding the rotor (or axle), or with the vehicle in park, crank the lug nut onto the stud with a socket and wrench. This seats the stud to the flange and you are ready to mount a wheel.

SETUP AND INSTALLATION

The axle assembly work begins when the differential components are fully disassembled, cleaned, and ready for reinstallation. If you are reusing the same ring and pinion gears and differential carrier, re-assembly is relatively simple because the mesh pattern does not have to be reset so the shims remain the same. Nothing really moves. If you're replacing the ring or pinion gears or the differential carrier, you have to start from the beginning for gear mesh and depth.

Before proceeding, verify that you have the correct parts. Check that the gears are actually the ratio that you ordered. This is the final safety check. Two main settings are critical to the operation of the axle assembly: pinion depth and backlash.

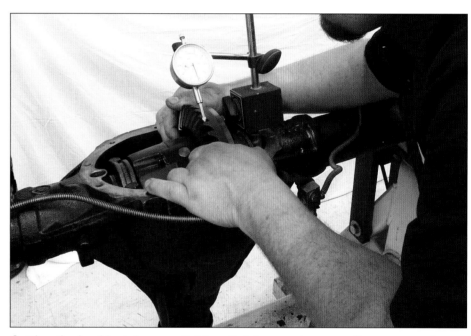

Setting the backlash is essential for attaining maximum performance and gear life from the ring and pinion gear. (Photo Courtesy Tony E. Huntimer)

Project: Installing an Axle Assembly and Differential

1 Measure Width of Shims

You use the same procedure for properly setting up the gears for a 10- or 12-bolt, regardless of the actual version you have. The only differences are a few of the settings specs, which vary by version and year. You start the procedure by setting pinion depth. You should begin by using the stock shim when installing a new pinion gear. Use a caliper micrometer to measure the width of the shims. It doesn't matter if you use one shim or five, just as long as they are clean and measure to the right spec.

Documentation Required

2 Calculate Pinion Depth

You need to correctly figure out the pinion depth and therefore the required shim stack. Two shims were used here to match the chosen spec, which for this 1969 12-bolt passenger car was set at .025 inch. The original shim was .020, the stock spec is .030, so I went in the middle, knowing that the previous setup was a little loose. The starting point is usually a rough guess between the factory spec and the previously installed shim.

3 Install Pinion

Following the procedure detailed in Chapter 6, install the pinion with the gear and bearing assembled and loaded into the housing.

4 Install Outer Pinion Bearing

To set the pinion depth, install a new outer pinion bearing, without a crush sleeve, over the new pinion shaft.

5 Lubricate Pinion Yoke Washer

Use gear oil to lubricate the original pinion yoke washer. You should also prelube the bearings.

Important!

6 Install Pinion Yoke

Use an impact wrench or ratchet to install the pinion yoke to the pinion. Be careful; there is no crush sleeve to take up the slack. The nut should be tightened slowly until the bearings contact the races and then tightened just a little bit more. Spin the yoke by hand; you should feel some drag. It should not be loose or tight.

7 Install Carrier

You have installed the new gears per Chapter 6. The carrier has new bearings, to which the new race and original shims are positioned.

8 Insert Carrier Assembly into Housing

Slide the assembly into the housing. You can feel whether it's a tight or loose fit within the case. If there is a certain amount of slop between the carrier bearing and the case, you need to add more shims. If it is too tight, try pushing the shims in after the carrier is in. If that doesn't work, you need thinner shims. This is all done by feel; pack in as many shims as you can.

Critical Inspection

9 Inspect Carrier Shims

You want the carrier shims as tight as possible. You can't get too much carrier bearing preload. If the carrier is loose or too tight, a new shim pack is in order.

10 Install Shims

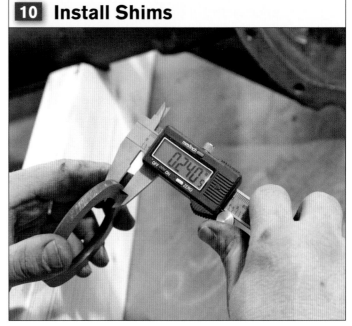

Use a caliper micrometer to measure the width of the shims. If your case needs more shims, measure the originals with calipers. Make sure they are clean, as any dirt or grease can change the reading.

11 Install Shims (CONTINUED)

The new shims are two-piece shells with an inner ridge for locating additional shims.

12 Install Shims (CONTINUED)

This is the outer shim shell. You can use any combination of shims to get the width you need.

13 Install Shims (CONTINUED)

The assembled shim pack locks together to facilitate installation.

14 Install Shims (CONTINUED)

You may use a stock shim on one side and a new shim on the other. This is just the initial alignment, you may need more.

Torque Fasteners

15 Torque Bearing Caps

To get the right pinion depth setting, torque the bearing caps to spec. Tighten both bolts until they are snug, then torque. Some housings have locating features for the caps. If this is the case, use a soft hammer to tap them into place first; don't use the bolts to pull them into place.

16 Lock Pinion Yoke to Platform

Working on the bench makes this process easier. Lock down the pinion yoke with a pair of bolts against a 2x4 platform.

17 Mount Dial Indicator on Housing

Position the dial indicator on the ring gear as inline as possible with the rotation of the gear. Refer to "Project: Setting Up a Dial Indicator" on page 105 for correct setup of the dial indicator. Zero the gauge with the ring gear pulled away from the gauge. Do this to set the initial backlash.

Precision Measurement

18 Measure Backlash

Rotate the gear forward until it contacts the pinion gear. With the pinion positively locked, this is easy. You want to be within the specs listed in this chapter. For the 12-bolt, the spec is .006 to .010 inch. This dial indicator reads .011, which is too loose. The shims need to be adjusted, more on the driver's side, less on the passenger's side, to move the carrier toward the passenger's side. One shim change will get it to .008 inch.

Pinion Depth

How deep or shallow the pinion gear rides in the housing is critical for proper mesh between the pinion and the ring gears. The factory specifies the starting point for the pinion shim, but this must usually be adjusted in or out to achieve the proper depth.

Too Deep

When the pinion gear is too deep in the ring gear, the mesh of the pinion teeth rides deep into the ring gear. This results in gear whine under acceleration. The solution is to move the pinion gear closer to the housing.

Too Shallow

If the pinion gear is too shallow, the gear mesh rides high on the ring gear teeth. This can result in a whine when the vehicle is decelerating. The solution is to move the pinion gear closer to the ring gear centerline.

There are two ways to set the pinion depth: with a pinion depth gauge and by checking the gear pattern. Both methods work; however, the pinion depth gauge is a bit cumbersome.

Pinion Gear Patterns

Pattern checking is the tried-and-true method of setting pinion depth. It is the process of installing the pinion gear (complete with inner and outer bearings), depth shims, pinion yoke, and pinion nut. However, you do not want to use a crush sleeve yet. You install the pinion gear and pull it tight with the pinion nut just until the bearings contact the races and there is no play. Then you install the carrier into the housing with the ring gear mounted.

Apply colored grease or gear-marking compound to a section of the ring gear. If the grease is too thick, you can mix it with a little oil to thin it. Gear-marking compound is designed for this specific task without running or smearing. Machinist's dye and other marking agents do not provide a clear contact patch and therefore it's difficult to interpret the contact patch.

Pinion Depth Gauge

Setting pinion depth is critical when rebuilding a Chevy 10- or 12-bolt differential. A variety of gauges are available. You can buy a simple economy gauge for about $30; the price and features increase from there to the elaborate and complicated versions that sell for hundreds of dollars.

Pinion depth tools are made specifically for Chevy 10- and 12-bolts, so they are not interchangeable. Positioned on the face of the installed pinion gear, they measure the depth of the pinion from the case, referencing the carrier bearing saddle. You must record the measurement and do some math to calculate the actual pinion depth. (Refer to the step-by-step procedures in Chapter 5.)

Although this is great for matching, the recommended depth number found on most aftermarket gears refers to the distance between the pinion gear end and the ring-gear centerline. The depth measurement is a reference and not an absolute number for every single housing. You need to ensure that the pinion and ring gear mesh correctly. To do that, you still have to check the gear pattern.

Pinion depth gauge tools work, and are effective for verifying pinion depth. However, using the suggested starting depths supplied in this chapter and checking your patterns is a simpler method that yields the same results. Ratech offers a pinion depth tool that is inexpensive and accurate.

Remember that the pinion-gear teeth need to be set at the correct distance in relation to the ring-gear teeth. Some inexpensive pinion depth tools measure from the carrier-bearing cap parting line, but the centerline often isn't the actual bearing centerline, and as a result, the measurement and gear mesh may be inaccurate. The Ratech pinion depth tool references the carrier bearing saddle at the bottom, and this is a far more accurate measurement point. Once the reference point is set, you divide the carrier-bearing diameter in half to determine the actual ring gear centerline, and therefore, the correct pinion depth. ∎

Project: Pattern Checking

1 Use Gear-Marking Compound

Once you set the initial backlash, check the mesh pattern. This shows the pinion depth in relation to the ring gear. You can thin the supplied gear-marking compound with a little gear oil.

2 Apply Gear-Marking Compound

Use a brush to apply the compound to several teeth in a couple of places along the ring gear. Try to make the compound smooth.

3 Allow Pinion to Rotate

Now the pinion is freed up, and one hand (or a helper) puts pressure on the pinion yoke while the other spins the ring gear several times in both directions.

4 Check Mesh Pattern

You can see where the pinion gear hypoid has contacted the ring gear. You want a center-weighted mesh. Checking the pattern requires close examination. This is an ideal pattern and about as good as it gets on the coast side.

5 Check Mesh Pattern *(CONTINUED)*

The drive side of this gear is also correct. You want smooth patterns; no sharp edges or saw-tooth shapes. Where the pattern falls on the gear heel to toe is not important; that is a function of the housing itself.

6 Check Mesh Pattern *(CONTINUED)*

Here is a bad pattern; the pinion is too close to the ring gear. Note the hard edge on the coast side; it looks like a shark fin. This would be very noisy and generate a lot of heat. The solution is a thinner pinion shim.

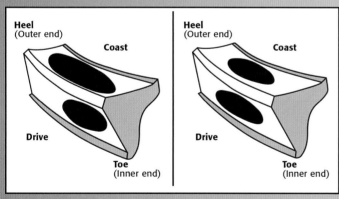

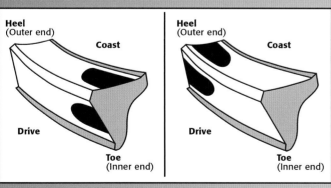

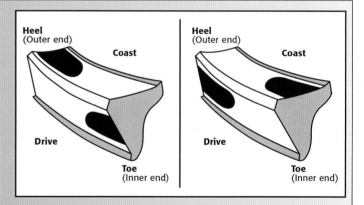

Here are examples of acceptable patterns. There should be no hard edges. The edges should look like rounded ink blots. Where the pattern falls on the gear heel to toe does not matter and cannot be easily changed.

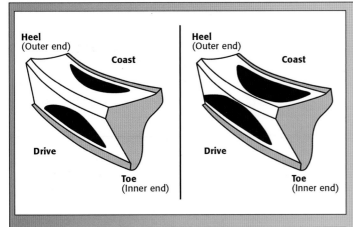

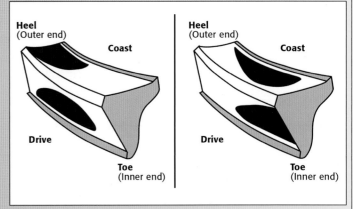

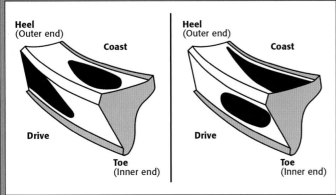

Note the hard edges at the root of the gear on these examples. This indicates that the pinion is too close to the ring gear. If one side is smooth and the other has sharp lines, it is still not acceptable. To correct, remove shims from the pinion gear. Work in small increments; big adjustments make really big movements.

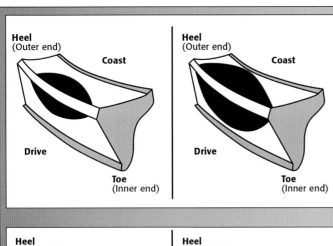

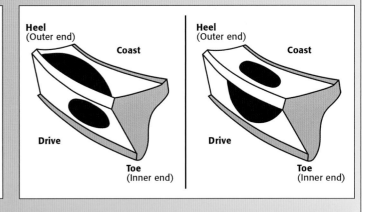

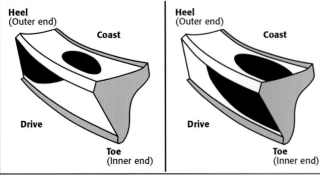

The pinion gear in these examples is not making clean contact with the ring gear, so the pattern is high on the teeth. To correct, add more shims to the pinion gear.

Rotate the carrier and not the pinion to check the contact patch. Use one hand to hold the pinion yoke, creating a load, and rotate the carrier four or five times in both directions. The pinion must have a load in it for the pattern to be accurate. (If holding it by hand is not feasible, wrap a shop towel around the yoke and pull it tight.) This shows the contact patch between the pinion gear and ring gear. Then read the pattern.

When reading the patterns for pinion depth, you should not be overly concerned about where pattern falls on the gear's heel and toe. Instead, you should focus on the position between the top land and root. Where the pattern lies heel to toe is dependent on the cut of the gears themselves and the left to right position of the ring gear carrier, as well as the housing itself. Trying to perfectly center the pattern is an exercise in futility. If the pattern is reasonably centered, it is sufficient.

The pattern should be checked at least twice during the installation procedure. First, an initial check should be done, and then the final check after the rebuild has been completed to make sure nothing has changed.

Acceptable Patterns

When the pinion depth is correct, the pattern shows smooth oval markings on both the coast and drive sides of the gear.

If the pinion is too close to the ring gear, the top of the gear pattern will be smooth and rounded, while the base of the pattern will be close to the root of the gear, cutting off in a sharp line. Certain patterns may show on one side as a teardrop or oval, with the other side cut off, even saw tooth–shaped.

If the pinion gear is too far away from the ring gear centerline, the pattern rides high on the teeth, showing a smooth rounded base with a sharp line on the top. Sometimes, there is one clean contact patch on drive or coast side, but the other side is cut off at the top.

Used Gears

Checking the pattern on used gear sets requires a different procedure. Ignore the drive side of the pattern; instead, concentrate on the coast pattern only. This is because the drive side already has wear from use, and the markings look like new patterns.

Project: Setting the Base Pinion Depth

1 To start, the pinion bearing needs to be pressed off the pinion. Any machine shop can do this for you for less than $10. Try to save the old bearing. Keep the original shim as well. If it is in good shape (not bent), it can be reused; otherwise you need to measure it with calipers and match it up with a new one from your installation kit.

If you have a hydraulic press, you can remove the bearing yourself using a bearing separator or a bearing clamshell. Pinion bearing removal requires a lot of pressure; you can't just beat the pinion out of the bearing with a hammer.

2 If the bearing came off the pinion in one piece, it can be reused for checking the pinion depth. Because you want to be able to remove the bearing to change the shims, the inner diameter of the bearing needs to be enlarged. You can do this with a die grinder and either a flap wheel or carbide cutting tool. Holding the bearing tightly in one hand (please wear gloves for this process), remove material evenly from the center of the bearing until it slides easily onto the new pinion gear.

3 If you are changing the gears, the pinion depth needs to be set. GM 10- and 12-bolt units use shims behind the inner pinion bearing (the large bearing inside the case).

Fortunately, you don't have to play the guessing game when it

Shim Specs

Here is a list of the factory shim depths for GM 10- and 12-bolt pinion gears.

10-Bolt

Differential	Pinion Depth (inch)	Differential	Pinion Depth (inch)
1963–1979 Corvette IRS	.030	8.2	.030
		8.25 IFS	.037
7.2	.030	8.5	.037
		8.6	.037

12-Bolt

Differential	Pinion Depth (inch)
Passenger Car and Truck	.030

comes to setting the pinion depth. The factory provides the pinion depth specs. You just need to do the final dial-in.

You can reuse the original shim or select a new shim that matches the factory specs. If there is a large difference between them, you can simply go with a shim that splits the difference. This occurs quite often, as the factory spec and the actual gears and housing do not always work together.

After the pinion depth has been set, use a hydraulic press to install the new bearing onto the pinion gear. If you don't have the special pinion tools, you can use a piece of heavy pipe and the old pinion bearing to match the size. Make sure the bearing is fully seated.

4 Place the shim on the pinion gear, and then slide on the bearing.

5 If you have not already installed new bearing races for the inner and outer pinion bearings, now is the time. *Do not* proceed with the original races in the housing.

6 Clean the pinion gear with brake cleaner or parts wash to remove any protective grease.

7 Slide the new pinion gear into the housing, install the outer pinion bearing and then the pinion yoke, followed by the pinion washer, and finally the original nut (if available). Do not install a crush sleeve at this time.

Sometimes the outer pinion bearing is very tight on the yoke, and has to be pushed onto the shaft with the pinion yoke. (This is a variance in the parts.)

Slowly thread the pinion nut onto the pinion, pulling the pinion bearings into their races. Once the bearings are fully seated and the pinion does not move in or out, apply a little more tension on the nut for a minimal amount of bearing preload. Remember, there is no

8 Install New Front Bearing

crush sleeve between the bearings, so too much load could damage the bearings.

The crush sleeve installs as shown, only after the pinion is in the housing. It rests between the inner bearing and the outer bearing inside the case. This image is for reference only, the sleeve is only installed after the pinion is in the case.

The new front bearing frequently fits quite tightly to the pinion bearing. You can use the yoke to help seat it if necessary.

Performance Tip

9 Install Front Bearing Seal

Once the bearing has been seated, install the new seal using a soft hammer or a seal driver. Passenger car 12-bolt seals are no longer available new, but the truck seal fits and works. Make sure that the seal is lubed with gear oil; otherwise it could tear.

10 Install Pinion Yoke

The yoke goes on next and then you place the thick yoke washer on the pinion. Not much thread is visible; this is normal, as the pinion may not slide easily onto the new pinion gear.

11 Install Pinion Yoke (CONTINUED)

Apply high-strength thread locker to the pinion threads before placing the new pinion.

12 Install Pinion Yoke (CONTINUED)

The best tool for this job is a 1/2-inch electric impact wrench. Hold the yoke by hand then crank on the nut until the bearings contact the races. Once they contact, work slowly until there is a slight drag on the yoke. It takes 300 to 400 ft-lbs to crush the sleeve. But once it crushes, it has to be right. Too much preload means starting over with a new sleeve.

13 Install Pinion Yoke (CONTINUED)

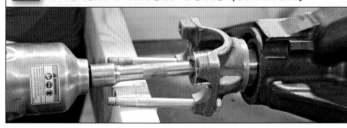

It can be difficult to apply the amount of torque required to crush the sleeve. Here the yoke is locked down on the bench. If you have to use a breaker bar, you can install an axle and either lock it down with a wrench or have a helper hold it in order to crush the sleeve.

Ring Gear Bolts

10-Bolt Differentials	Factory Torque (ft-lbs)
1963–1979 Corvette IRS	55
7.2	55
8.2	55
8.25 IFS	65
8.5	65
8.6	65
12-Bolt Differentials	Factory Torque (ft-lbs)
Passenger Car and Truck	55

14 Next, the carrier and the gear should be cleaned with brake cleaner or parts wash to remove any protective grease.

15 If you have not replaced the bearings on the carrier, now is the time to do it. The ring gear should drop right onto the carrier, and; with just a little effort, seat onto the gear flange. Secure two bolts to the ring gear and thread them in by hand.

Apply a small amount of thread locker to the rest of the bolts and thread them into the gear. Remove the two bolts used to secure the gear in position and apply threadlocker. Reinstall the bolts.

If you have an assistant, have him (or her) hold the carrier. If not, you can use a bench vise. The ring gear bolts must be torqued in a criss-cross star pattern to ensure that the gear is properly seated and torqued.

16 During disassembly, you removed and labeled the carrier preload shims. Retrieve them and prepare them for installation. If you are reusing the original carrier, it should work as is.

17 Check Pinion Preload

Once the preload is close by feel, check it with an inch-pound torque wrench. You need a wrench that measures 0 to 20 in-lbs in 1-inch increments. These are small and usually have a 1/4-inch drive. You can see the shop-made tool that adapts a 1/4-inch drive to a 1/2-inch socket. The large adapter shown here is a 3/4- to 1/2-inch adapter with a small 1/4-inch socket welded to the inside. It works.

18 Check Pinion Preload *(CONTINUED)*

Without axles installed, rotate and measure the yoke. The initial torque is not the spec you want; rather, it's the rotational force needed to spin it. The measurement here is 6 in-lbs, which is within spec for used bearings, but new bearings need to be 14 to 19. Once the preload is set, you can use a punch to tap the pinion nut to help keep it from backing off.

19 Install the carrier into the housing and hold it in position with one hand and use the other hand to slide the preload shims into the housing between the carrier bearings and the case. They should be tight, but not so tight that they don't slide in.

If you are using a new carrier, you may have to adjust the shim package. As long as the carrier is not loose side to side, the originals should be sufficient for this process. Replace the carrier end caps and torque them to spec, which is 60 ft-lbs for all GM 10- and 12-bolt units.

20 Mix up a little gear-marking compound and follow the procedure for marking the ring gear and check the pattern (see "Project: Pattern Checking" on page 98). In the unlikely event that the pattern is dead-on this time around, pat yourself on the back. This does not happen often. More likely, you will need a series of trial-and-error test fittings. Once you have a baseline pattern, you can adjust it.

You want to make large changes that intentionally move the pinion to the other extreme so you can see which direction you need to move (if you are too close, push the pinion deeper, or vice versa). Once the pattern is in the ballpark, you can make small adjustments to fine-tune it. A large adjustment is .005 to .015 inch, and small changes are .002 to .004 inch. If you start out making small adjustments, the process takes much longer. As you reach the correct pattern, the smaller adjustments center the pattern between the top and root of the gear teeth.

21 Once you reach the correct pinion depth, remove the pinion gear from the housing and install the new inner bearing to the pinion gear with the correct shims. This can be done with a basic hydraulic press and a piece of heavy-wall pipe or a bearing clamshell. If you don't have the ability to do this in your shop, any local machine shop can install the bearing for you. Remember, do not install the new bearing until you are sure that the pinion depth is correct.

Ring Gear Backlash

Next in the process of setup is setting the initial backlash for the ring gear. This is the amount of forward and backward headspace between the ring gear and pinion. Backlash is measured with the pinion gear installed in the housing, with minimal preload. You need a dial indicator with a magnetic base to check the backlash.

Backlash is adjusted by moving the carrier left or right with shims between the carrier bearings and the axle assembly housing. Moving the carrier to the right (passenger's side) pushes the ring gear into the pinion, decreasing backlash. Moving the carrier to the left (driver's side) away from the carrier, increases backlash.

Most gear sets follow these basic parameters: Moving .010 inch toward the pinion gear yields a decrease of .007 inch in backlash. Moving .010 inch away from the pinion

gear yields an increase of .007 inch in backlash. The sweet spot for GM 10- and 12-bolt backlash is between .006 and .010 inch. If the backlash is too tight, the gears generate a lot of heat and burn up. If the backlash is too loose, the gears are clunky and noisy.

Almost all factory carriers are shimmed with a solid spacer that has been machined specifically for that housing. If you retain the carrier, it may work great, but it usually needs adjustment. A shim kit that includes

a pair of master spacers and a series of shims of varying thicknesses does the trick. The master spacers lock together in the center and hold the shims in the pack, making installation easier. The shim pack also provides the carrier bearing preload, but that is the last step.

For now, you want the shim pack to be snug, but not tight. Use calipers to measure the original spacer and select shims from the kit to match. Try this first and add or remove shims from there.

Project: Setting the Ring Gear Backlash

1 Install the carrier into the housing, and then slide the shim packs between the bearing races and the housing. Bolt the end caps in place and torque to spec, 60 ft-lbs per bolt. Set up your dial indicator, taking care that it measures near 90 degrees to the ring gear (see "Project: Setting Up a Dial Indicator" below).

2 Secure the pinion yoke from moving; this is a key compo-

nent to checking backlash. If possible, mechanically secure the pinion so that it can't move at all. Rotate the carrier until it contacts the pinion gear, and then zero the gauge on the indicator. The indicator dial can be zeroed anywhere on the dial.

3 Once the zero point is determined, rotate the carrier in the opposite direction until it contacts the pinion gear again. Read the dial.

If the measurement is between .006 and .010 inch, you are good to go. If not, the shim pack must be adjusted until the correct backlash range is reached. Once you find the correct shim load, check the backlash in at least three places on the ring gear to be certain it is correct.

4 Record the shim sizes for each side, just in case you need to rebuild the shim pack.

Project: Setting Up a Dial Indicator

Proper setup of the dial indicator is crucial for getting accurate measurements. In the case of reading backlash, you need one with a magnetic base. This allows you to position the indicator anywhere there is a ferrous (magnetic) surface. The Summit Racing kit shown here costs about $30. A typical kit will contain the indicator, the magnetic base, a couple of adjustable arms, and a case. As long as the unit is accurate to .001 inch, it will work for this task.

The magnetic base must be stable and locked to the housing. If it moves at all, the measurements will

not be accurate. In addition, you need to properly tighten the clamps. Loose clamps mean the indicator can move when pressure is put on the

needle and the gauge's readings will be inaccurate.

Of course, the gauge needs to be properly zeroed. Don't zero the gauge

Dial indicators are very useful for all kinds of automotive measurement work, but they are critical for setting up a differential.

at the actual end of the gauge's movement because this can lead to false readings as well. Push the needle in a bit and then zero the scale to that point. This allows you to get an accurate reading at the true zero point.

Make sure you double-check your readings. The large indicator scale has hash marks in .001-inch increments. A smaller second gauge indicates tenths of an inch, up to 1 inch.

The indicator's scale rotates on the gauge. Don't worry about tightening the lock knob. The scale is not loose on the gauge; it won't move. The act of tightening the knob can take the gauge out of position. The magnet on the base is strong, but it slides easily with moderate pressure.

To properly position the indicator on the housing to take readings, follow these steps.

1 Install Magnetic Base

A magnetic base is the first part of the indicator. Your kit must include one for ease of securing it to the housing. You can mount the dial indicator on any part of the center section that is clear of your work area.

2 Mount Second Arm

The second arm slides onto the base's flagpole. You can slide it up and down as necessary.

3 Mount Second Arm (CONTINUED)

The mount on the back of the indicator attaches to the second arm. Install this loosely until the final adjustment is complete.

4 Mount Dial Indicator on Housing

The base has an on/off lever that moves the magnets to the base to secure it to the housing. The base also has a V shape on the bottom for round surfaces.

5 Mount Dial Indicator on Housing *(CONTINUED)*

An adjustable angle fitting on the second arm helps get the indicator in the best position.

6 Mount Dial Indicator on Housing *(CONTINUED)*

This is a good position for taking the backlash reading. The base is solid and not wobbly and the indicator is inline with the ring gear. You want to read the gear with the indicator inline with the rotation of the gear.

7 Position Gauge Needle

The needle of the gauge should sit on the edge of the tooth without slipping off.

8 Zero the Gauge

Once the indicator is positioned, it has to be zeroed. The outer ring of the gauge rotates so that you can set the "0" mark where ever it needs to be. Each hash-mark is .001 inch. Move the ring slowly so you don't throw off the alignment.

Preload Adjustments

Once the pinion depth and backlash have been set, check the gear pattern again. If all is well, you can move on to adjusting carrier bearing preload and pinion bearing preload, as well as installing crush sleeves. Apply a coating of fresh gear oil to the bearings before proceeding with the final installation.

Carrier Bearing Preload

The carrier bearings must have some load on them for the unit to operate correctly. All GM 10- and 12-bolt housings use an outside shim design for the carrier bearings. After the backlash has been set, add equal shims to both sides until the preload is as tight as possible without damaging the shims. Carrier bearings rarely fail because of too much preload; in fact, it is difficult to load too many shims in this design without using tools. The shims should be tight, and it may help to pack the shims with the carrier halfway out of the housing and roll the assembly into position all at once.

Pinion Bearing Preload

This is the most critical component of the final assembly, and the GM design uses a crush sleeve, which is the trickiest of them all. The pinion preload is achieved by tightening the pinion nut until the bearings contact the races and then continue loading the bearings until they have reached a range of rotational torque that is measured in in-lbs.

Many experienced axle assembly builders don't use a gauge for this; instead, they rely on their sense of feeling for the right range. Although this works for the experienced builder, the novice should rely on the proper tools to get the job done right. Too much preload kills bearings; not enough makes for a noisy ride.

Crush Sleeves

This is a special metal sleeve that crushes with 300 to 400 ft-lbs of torque. That means that to properly set the pinion bearing preload, you need to put that amount of force onto the pinion nut. If you are working under the car on the ground, this task is not easy without an impact wrench. Many air-impact wrenches are not capable of this kind of torque; you need at least a 1/2-inch-drive impact, if not a 3/4-drive unit. Electric impact wrenches can provide the torque you need. You have to have the right tool for the job before you start.

If the vehicle is on a lift or the pieces are on the bench, you can use a breaker bar with a long pipe to achieve the best results. This is the hardest part of any 10- or 12-bolt rebuild, simply because of the torque required.

Installing crush sleeves requires a lot of patience and finesse. If you overload the bearings, you can't just back off the torque; you need a new crush sleeve. Most rebuild kits come with two crush sleeves for this reason.

You must check the preload several times as you tighten the pinion nut. If you use an impact wrench, watch the socket for movement as you hit the trigger. As you reach the point of preload, the socket does not move much; use very small increments. Check the preload often, until it reaches the range for your unit.

Pinion Bearing Spacer Kits

Although the factory design uses crush sleeves, you can use an aftermarket spacer and shim kit instead. This removes the potential for ruining crush sleeves by replacing the sleeve with a solid spacer and a set of shims. The best thing about these kits is that the results are easily reproduced every time you remove the pinion from the center section, as long as you use the same shims.

To increase preload, you remove shims; to reduce preload, you add shims. You determine the correct shim pack for the preload range for your axle assembly by using the trial-and-error method of adding and removing shims.

Bearing Sizes		
10-Bolt	*New Bearing*	*Used Bearing*
1963–1979 Corvette IRS	14 to 19	6 to 8
7.2	11 to 14	6 to 7
8.2	12 to 15	6 to 7
8.25 IFS	14 to 19	6 to 8
8.5	14 to 19	6 to 8
8.6	14 to 19	6 to 8
12-Bolt	*New Bearing*	*Used Bearing*
Passenger Car	14 to 19	6 to 8
Truck	13 to 15	6 to 7

One key point on installing pinion spacer kits: Make sure that the spacer and the shims are very clean. Any dirt or dust on the surface can affect the preload measurements. These kits are available for most GM axle assembly designs.

Complete the Rebuild

Once you have set up the ring and pinion, you install the rest of the components, starting with the axles. The outer axle bearings, or wheel bearings, should be replaced (see Chapter 6 for more details).

Lubricate the axle seals with grease or gear oil. Skipping this step could result in a torn seal, which means a big mess and having to tear down the housing to fix it.

The axles slide into the housing; take care not to gouge the seal. Once the axle ends reach the carrier, the splines must be rotated until they slide into the carrier. With both axles in place, push them as far as they will go toward the carrier.

Before you install the axles and the rear cover fill the housing with new gear oil.

Unless you are working with a Buick or Olds 8.2 or 8.5 10-bolt, the axles are retained by a C-clip. Slip the original C-clips (or replacements if the originals are unavailable) into the groove in the axle. Once the clip is in, pull the axle outward, locking the clip in place. Repeat for the other side. With both C-clips in place, reinstall the cross-shaft and cross-shaft retainer bolt.

The housing is now ready to be reinstalled into the vehicle.

Cover and Fluid

The differential cover must be sealed to the housing. You can use a paper gasket, RTV silicone, or a combination of the two; any of these methods is sufficient. As long as the housing and cover are clean, you should get a leak-free seal. If the rear cover is tweaked or bent at all, a paper gasket will likely leak.

Most builders apply a light coat of silicone to both sides of the gasket and then install the cover to the housing.

The cover bolts are next. Thread them into the housing and torque them to spec in a star-pattern. If you are using an aluminum cover, snug all of the bolts first and then torque to 20 ft-lbs.

Use the new gasket provided in your kit. If you don't have a gasket, silicone works too.

Differential Support Covers

Installing a support cover is an available upgrade. Unlike dress-up covers, a support cover actually serves a purpose other than simply looking good. Typically made of cast aluminum, these lightweight covers feature carrier pinion pre-load bolts.

They add support to the open side of the housing and this makes a big difference in controlling rearward deflection of the differential. In most cases, just 5 ft-lbs does the trick.

Most support covers also have other features, such as cooling fins to reduce the internal temperature of the gear oil, which prolongs the

Fancy chrome covers certainly look good under a car or truck, but they don't have any performance benefit.

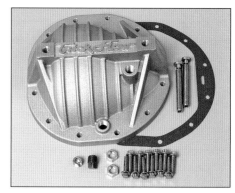

This rear-end girdle from Trick Flow does several things to help your differential. The preload screws keep the differential caps from pushing out under heavy loads. The two extra holes in the middle and bottom of the cover are a fill port and a drain plug for easier servicing.

Before reinstalling the rear cover, the old gasket and silicone must be cleaned off. Make sure it is clean, as a leaky rear end is a time bomb.

life of the gears and bearings, as well as a small increase in fluid capacity. For high-torque applications, such as off-road and drag racing, these covers can make a big difference in longevity.

Gear Oil

The manufacturer of the differential inside your housing makes the decision for you regarding which gear oil to use. That said, there are still a lot of choices to be made.

Modern gear oils are designed specifically for use in manual transmissions and axle assemblies. Gears have specific durability issues, such as work hardening, pitting, spalling, and scoring that must be taken into consideration when designing a lubricant. Additives are blended into the base oil to provide protection against these and other gear-specific issues.

You need to choose the correct viscosity for your gear oil. SAE (Society of Automotive Engineers) and API (American Petroleum Institute) provide an oil viscosity rating, which is based on the oil's ability to resist flowing at specific temperatures.

SAE rating labels are in a format you have seen many times, such as 10W-30 or 75W-90.

Straight-weight oils are measured at 100 degrees Celsius, while multi-grade oils (anything with a "W" in the grade) are measured for a specific viscosity at multiple temperatures.

Multi-grade lubricants feature special modifiers that allow the molecules to alter how they react at different temperatures as the oil thins. This allows a single oil to cover a wider range of temperatures and working conditions.

The API ratings are not classified by viscosity, but rather by usage.

Although some gear manufacturers may suggest a different grade, choose your manufacturer's recommendation for the grade for your differential carrier. This ensures that you have the best oil for the application.

The rating of GL-1 is intended for manual transmissions in mild conditions without additives or modifiers. GL-2 is used for worm-gear axles, which are not commonly found in automotive use. GL-3 is for severe-load manual transmission usage. It is not intended for hypoid gear use. GL-4 is for hypoid gears in moderate duty and load. Ring and pinion manufacturers commonly specify it. GL-5 is the most commonly used type for differentials; it is rated for hypoid gears in high-speed heavy shock loads and low-speed high-torque loads. This is what most differentials see, especially high-performance applications. MT-1 is rated for non-synchronized manual transmissions. It is used in heavy-duty vehicles such as buses and industrial trucks.

Friction Modifiers

If your differential is a clutch-type LSD, you need to add a friction modifier. These are designed to reduce chatter and provide longer life for the clutches. Without it, clutches are noisy and do not function as well as they could. The rule of thumb is to add 2 ounces per quart of gear oil; that's 4 percent for used clutches, and up to 8 percent for new clutches. Adding more does not really help, and in some instances hurts the overall effect.

Always consult the manual for your aftermarket differential when it comes to adding LSD friction modifiers to the gear oil.

Gear Break-In Procedure

Drag racers tell you that there is no break-in period for gears. Well, for *them*, there is no break-in period. The only distance their vehicle travels is 1/4 mile of hard throttle, and then a 1/2-mile leisurely cruise back to the pits. There is not enough time for the oil to heat up and cause any issues. However, for street and off-road vehicles, nothing could be further from reality. New bearings are nice and tight, but that also means heat. Heat is what kills gears.

The most important time for a new set of gears is the first 500 miles. This is when the first heat cycles are made, and the wear patterns are established. Here are the established rules for gear break-in:

- First 15 miles: Keep the speed under 60 mph. Allow the gears to cool for 30 minutes before driving farther. Repeat until 100 miles have been traveled.
- Avoid heavy throttle, hard starts, and high speeds during the first 500 miles. After the first 100 miles, long trips are fine, but avoid high speeds for the remaining 400 miles.

Here is the advice that was provided by a major gear manufacturer after a fresh build two days before a long road trip that culminated in an evening of drag racing: "Just run the gears. Don't worry about burning them up. If you did a good job putting the gears and differential together, there are not going to be any issues. Problems with gear installs usually show up in the first 100 miles, so just go out, drive the car like you stole it, and don't worry about."

Those are words to live by.

DRIVESHAFTS

In any rear-wheel-drive car, the driveshaft is one common link between the transmission and the rear differential. The driveshaft in most vehicles is a single-piece unit, with a U-joint at either end. Although it's vital, it is just a piece of steel or aluminum tubing and there is not that much science behind it. In reality, the driveshaft is critical for coupling the drivetrain together; it can also prevent power from reaching the tires and make driving the car a nightmare if it isn't properly designed.

Choosing a Builder

Although driveshaft design is important, the manner in which it is built is equally as important. A design is only as good as the workmanship that goes into putting it together. Building the right driveshaft for the application is critical.

If you're building a high-performance vehicle, you should get a professionally built driveshaft from a good driveline shop. If you are going to have a local driveshaft shop build your driveshaft, you need to be prepared to provide all vital information and measurements to build the driveshaft.

The shop needs to stand behind its work and rebuild the driveshaft if necessary. Make sure you tell them it is for a high-performance application, which is very different from a stock driveshaft; it needs to be built to a higher standard. Ordering a driveshaft on the Internet from a reputable high-performance builder is not only easy, but also guaranteed.

Power Output Considerations

Any increase in the power output of an engine has a direct effect on the driveshaft. As the power output increases, however, the detrimental effects increase as well. Typically, the factory driveshaft is balanced between 3,000 and 3,500 rpm. When the driveshaft's RPM goes beyond that range, the driveshaft experiences parasitic losses that eat up horsepower.

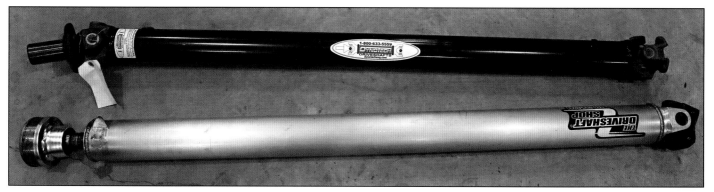

Dynotech Engineering offers a variety of driveshafts for almost any application. In fact, Dynotech offers composite, aluminum, steel, and hybrid driveshafts. A steel DOM 3-1/2-inch driveshaft (top) and a 4-inch aluminum driveshaft (bottom) are shown here.

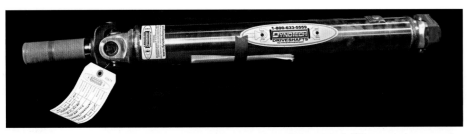

The driveshaft connects the transmission to the differential. When you upgrade the differential, it is good idea to examine the driveshaft, especially if you have added horsepower.

According to Steve Raymond of DynoTech Engineering, a properly balanced driveshaft can save 3 to 7 hp on a chassis dyno. "That's why balance is important and why we manufacture shafts for about 85 to 90 percent of the NASCAR teams," Raymond told me. The stock balance on a stock driveshaft is not good enough for anything but a stock engine.

Balancing

DynoTech Engineering uses Balance Engineering driveshaft balancers that deliver superior balancing accuracy. Balancing a performance driveshaft to at least 5,000 rpm ensures proper tuning and drastically reduces parasitic loss. Some applications are balanced as high as 7,500 rpm.

Slip Yoke Measurement

The length and diameter of the driveshaft are very important to the overall performance of the unit. The most important distance is from the rear yoke to the transmission seal. This must be measured with the car

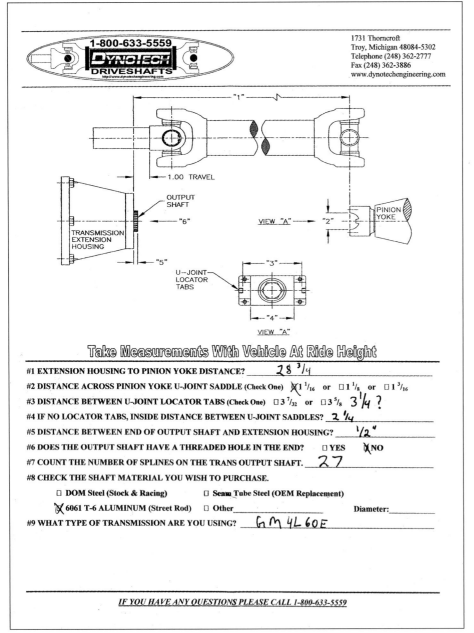

This is an example of the order sheet for a new shaft. You need to provide complete information.

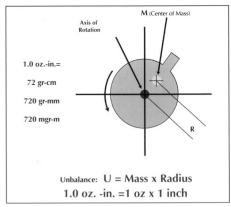

This illustration shows the internal mechanics of balancing. As the shaft rotates, the mass center and the rotational center are different. Adding weight in the correct areas brings these points together. (Illustration Courtesy Dynotech Engineering)

If you are changing the housing or transmission, it is important to check the angles of both the pinion yoke and the transmission output shaft. This magnetic angle finder is the best way to do it. You want the transmission to have a downward angle of 1 to 5 degrees; 2 is optimum. This is usually not easily adjustable, unless you are swapping transmissions.

The pinion yoke should be set at ride height with an upward angle of 1 to 5 degrees. The two angles should be within a degree of each other.

at ride height with the pinion yoke installed. Changing to a billet pinion yoke can alter the length by as much as 3/4 inch, for example.

The driveshaft shop builds the shaft with the required slip yoke and runout. Take the slip yoke measurement carefully and methodically. It is the length of the splined yoke section that sticks out of the transmission at resting ride height.

Because this measurement must be made at resting ride height, you have to get under the car. The best method is to place jack stands under the axle assembly and front suspension. Make sure the stands are all at the same height. The slightest variation in the suspension can throw off the measurement, resulting in a driveshaft that does not fit. Don't just jack up the rear and leave the front wheels on the ground because it can skew the measurements, and then you may get the wrong-length driveshaft.

For most applications, a runout of 1 inch is more than enough to provide the play needed for suspen-

sion travel. Unless you are running an off-road vehicle or air/hydraulic suspension that has large amounts of travel, the standard 1-inch runout is best. Runout of more than 1 inch is too much. Some transmission shops may try to convince you that 1.5 inches is required. *Do not* buy into it. That much runout could leave you with less than 3 inches of spline section in the transmission, which allows the yoke to wobble on the

output shaft, resulting in a heavy vibration at various RPM.

Critical Speed

Proper driveshaft length helps yield the best diameter. Critical speed is the RPM at which the driveshaft becomes unstable and flexes in the middle or "jump ropes."

The longer and smaller (diameter) a driveshaft, the slower its critical speed. Critical speed is felt as

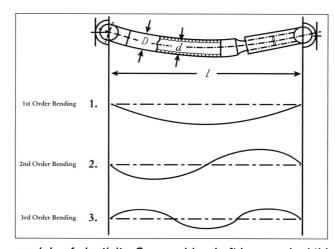

Drivelines experience three types of bending. The potential issues are the loss of power and eventual failure of the shaft. As the RPM increases, all driveshafts reach their critical speed and start to flex. The amount of flex depends on the speed and length of the driveshaft, and the module of elasticity. Once a driveshaft has reached third-order bending, failure is imminent. The driveshaft has been subjected to enormous stress and sometimes it breaks before this stage. (Illustration Courtesy Dynotech Engineering)

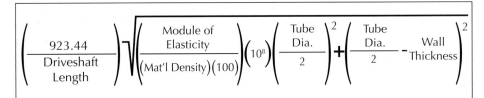

$$\left(\frac{923.44}{\text{Driveshaft Length}}\right)\sqrt{\frac{\text{Module of Elasticity}}{(\text{Mat'l Density})(100)}\left(10^8\right)\left(\frac{\text{Tube Dia.}}{2}\right)^2+\left(\frac{\text{Tube Dia.}}{2}-\text{Wall Thickness}\right)^2}$$

The formula for calculating critical speed is fairly complex. This is included for reference only as the module of elasticity is regarded as a trade secret, and each material is different.

excessive vibration, and if the shaft is run at or above critical speed for too long, the unit fails.

Calculating the critical speed requires the length, diameter, wall thickness, and the material module of elasticity figures for the shaft.

Material

The build material of the driveshaft makes a difference. Factory steel driveshafts are really only suitable for OEM power. Most OEM shafts are rated for up to 350 ft-lbs of torque or 350 to 400 hp. If the factory shaft is a two-piece unit for a vintage Mustang, it cannot handle even that amount of torque because a rubber sleeve holds together the two pieces of the driveshaft. Factory aluminum driveshafts, such as those found in Fox-Body cars, have similar ratings.

High-performance driveshafts are available in several materials: drawn-over-mandrel (DOM) steel, chrome-moly steel, aluminum, and carbon fiber. DOM seamless tubing is stronger than OEM steel, capable of supporting 1,300 ft-lbs and 1,300 hp. DOM steel has a higher RPM rating as well. This is a good budget choice for any car that does not require a lighter shaft.

Going to chrome-moly steel, which is the strongest possible material, is a major step. Pro Stock cars run chrome-moly driveshafts. Heat-treating chrome-moly steel tubing increases the torsional strength by 22 percent, and increases the critical speed by 19 percent. Chrome-moly steel is heavy, though, which is a problem because it increases the load on the engine.

The next step is to CNC weld each shaft for a perfect joint. (Photo Courtesy Dynotech Engineering)

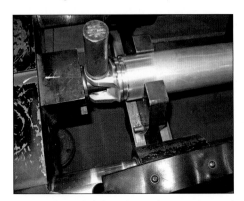

These metal yokes have been pressed into the aluminum tubing in the correct phasing. (Photo Courtesy Dynotech Engineering)

Once the yoke has cooled from welding, the shaft is assembled and balanced. This is a state-of-the-art balancer, and it is unlikely that your local driveshaft shop has one so you need to find a specialist for the job. (Photo Courtesy Dynotech Engineering)

Eliminating weight is important. Lighter materials, even if they are not as strong, are sometimes a better choice. Aluminum is the most common performance driveshaft material. A lightweight aluminum shaft reduces rotational mass, which in turn decreases parasitic loss. Aluminum driveshafts are quite strong, handling up to 900 ft-lbs and 1,000 hp. This is not as much as DOM steel, but if you are making 500 hp, the weight savings alone is worth it.

For the ultimate in light weight, you can choose carbon fiber. Tubes made from carbon fiber are expensive, but also are efficient. Capable of 1,200 ft-lbs and 900 to 1,500 hp, carbon fiber is a great choice. Carbon fiber also has an incredibly high torsional strength, which helps lower the shock to the axle assembly. Carbon-fiber shafts do not flex much, and have a high module of elasticity. A carbon-fiber driveshaft combines the highest critical speed factors, and its light weight frees up as much as 5 hp over a steel driveshaft. When winning is everything, 5 hp might make the difference.

Carrier Bearings

If you are building a truck or a very long vehicle, a carrier bearing might be necessary. A carrier bearing uses two shorter shafts instead of one long shaft. One half is a stationary unit that only rotates; it is in a fixed position to the transmission and the carrier unit. The other half uses a slip yoke that slides into the carrier bearing unit and mounts to the differential.

Most full-size trucks use carrier bearings to minimize vibrations and reduce the overall diameter of the driveshaft. They are not as strong as a one-piece unit. The two-piece shaft has twice as many connections and U-joints so the opportunities for failure are twice as high.

Some smaller cars used two-piece driveshafts from the factory, such as the X-frame Biscayne. Swapping to a single-piece shaft is easy and yields excellent results.

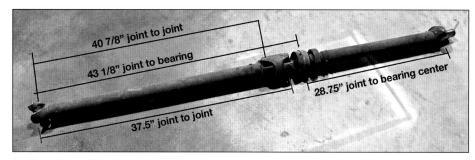

Multi-piece driveshafts can be complex, especially older ones such as this one from a mid-1960s Buick B-Body. This type includes a carrier bearing and a double U-joint in the center. Before ordering a new shaft, take some photos of the old shaft and make notes of the measurements on it so you can send this information to the driveshaft shop.

Corvettes need bolt-in slip yokes because the transmission crossmember is not removable.

You need to match the inside slip yoke to the transmission output shaft. Full engagement of the slip yoke into the transmission with 1 inch of run-out is necessary for proper fitment.

The pinion yoke bolts to the pinion gear. The U-joint must match the driveshaft; if they don't match, you have to change one of them. Stock yokes are suitable for mild performance, but 500-plus–hp vehicles should use high-performance yokes.

The 12-bolt truck pinion yoke has a built-in seal. The seal on the housing must match the yoke. The pinion yoke must also match the pinion gear and the housing for correction installation.

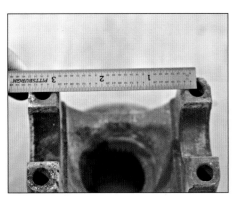

Proper measurements are critical for selecting components. You find the width of the yoke by measuring from the center of one bolt hole to the center of the other bolt hole.

The slip yoke and the pinion yoke are crucial points of failure in the driveline. They represent the connection points between the tranny, driveshaft, and differential. When this component fails, all hell breaks loose. A driveshaft can snap in the middle of the splines. Although this type of failure is rare, it does happen. A cast yoke is strong enough to handle approximately 800 hp, depending on the setup. A lightweight car with street tires puts less stress on the driveline than a 2-ton muscle car with a blown big-block and slicks.

U-Joint

Phasing in the U-joint with the yokes is an area that smaller shops might not pay much attention to. This is where using a pro shop is important. Every rotation at which the joint is beyond 0 degrees produces a fourth-order vibration. Proper phasing of the yokes to decrease the combined degree of rotation limits this vibration.

No component in the driveline is insignificant, including the U-joint.

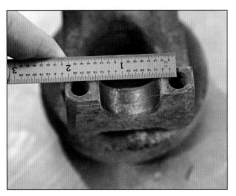

Measure across the bearing caps between the centers of the bolt holes to determine the correct size of U-joint.

A greasable joint has a hollow body and must be serviced occasionally, such as with every other oil change. It is important that these joints receive grease on a regular basis. This is also an adapter joint with large bearing caps on one side and small caps on the other side.

Not only is the brand of joint important, so is the style. Although load capacity is important, there are other factors to consider. Just about every domestic mid-size car uses the 1310-series U-joint. For performance and heavy-duty use, a 1350-series joint is ideal. As the series number increases, so does the size of the trunnion (the protruding shafts that the caps cover) diameter, which yields more torsional strength. Torsional forces are exerted in rotation.

This solid Spicer U-joint is non-greasable and is the strongest one available. There is grease inside the joint, but you can't add more. These actually last longer than greasable joints, so don't be concerned about that.

Swapping a U-joint is not difficult, but if you have not done it before, it can be frustrating.

Changes here are not to be made lightly; you can't just pop in a bigger-series U-joint. All of the yokes, whether slip-, bolt-, or weld-in, must match. However, there are crossover U-joints that allow you run half of one size, and half of another size. This is good for interim projects and junkyard swaps if the two components don't match up.

U-joints are available with different body types: solid or greasable. The Spicer-style solid-body U-joint does not require periodic greasing, and does not have zerk fittings for grease. These units are stronger than the typical greasable U-joint because the bodies are solid rather than hollow. The solid body provides much

more strength than greasable joints, which can twist and break under severe loads.

Mounting Options

General Motors employed several methods to secure the U-joints. The most common design is a set of spring clips, which have inner and outer styles.

Staking

Commonly found on newer vehicles, the caps and yoke are permanently locked together by pressing a series of deforming punches around the outer perimeter of the cap to the yoke interface. These joints are not

rebuildable; the entire shaft must be replaced when the joints go bad. They are not common to GM vehicles.

Nylon Injection

This is a typical retaining method for many GM driveshafts, dating back to the 1960s. These joints are bonded to the yoke with a molten plastic. It is injected into the yoke via a channel in both the yoke and the cap. When the joint goes bad, the plastic must be melted or sheared in order to remove the U-joint.

Removal Methods

Two main types of driveshafts were used on early GM vehicles:

U-Joint Terminology

U-joints have several components, each with several key aspects relative to both their design and installation.

Bearing Cup

This is the part of the U-joint that mounts into the yokes. It is filled with grease and roller bearings.

Bearing Cup Seal

This keeps the U-joint sealed from dirt and contaminants; the seals are located at the end of each bearing cap. These are usually rubber, but can also be hard plastic.

Flange Yoke

If your differential, transmission, or transfer case uses a bolt-in yoke, it is called a flange yoke.

Journal Cross

The main body of the U-joint is called the journal cross. It may be solid or filled with grease, depending on the type of joint.

Needle Bearings

Just as the name suggests, thin barrel-shaped bearings are pressed against the inside of the U-joint cap. You have to

watch these little guys because they like to fall out of place and keep the cap from fully seating. If you have ever shattered a U-joint, you have likely seen them all over the ground.

Propshaft Yoke

If the yoke is welded to the driveshaft tube, it is called a propshaft yoke or a weld-on yoke.

Slip Yoke

The transmission end of the driveshaft has inner splines that slide in and out of the transmission as the axle assembly moves up and down. This is called a slip yoke. These can also be found on two-piece driveshafts and transfer cases.

Snap Ring

These come it two styles: inner and outer; they are used to secure the U-joint to the yoke.

Thrust Washer

Some U-joint caps have a small washer, the thrust washer, on the inside of the cap to control the width of the U-joint.

Trunnion

The trunnion is the stub on the end of the journal cross. The needle bearings ride on the trunnion. ■

Saginaw and Dana, named for the companies that made them. The Saginaw shafts use nylon injection and the Dana shafts use snap rings. Removing the U-joints from nylon-injected caps requires either heat or pressure.

Heat

This is the most common method of removing the plastic. The key is to limit the heat to the U-joint and not to get the yoke red hot. A propane torch is the best option here, as propane doesn't burn hot enough to overheat the yoke. With the shaft positioned securely, use the torch to heat the caps. Once the plastic melts, it begins to come out of the hole in the yoke like little plastic worms. Don't be alarmed if the grease catches fire; this is normal. Once the plastic is melted, you can press out the caps relatively easily.

Pressure

The other option is to use high pressure to shear the plastic off. Unless you have a hydraulic press, you will have some difficulty removing the caps with this method, as it takes several thousand pounds of force to shear the plastic. Another caveat for this method is that you can damage the yoke if it is not properly supported under the press with a socket or cup that has an inner diameter just larger than the bearing cup itself. If the yoke is deformed, replacement is the only option.

Once the old joint is out, the new joint can be installed using the inner snap ring method (see below).

Project: Installing a Driveshaft U-Joint

1 Remove Locking Pin

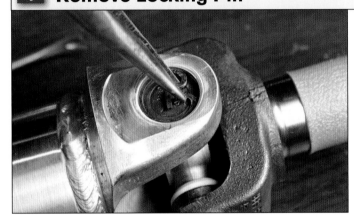

Remove the locking pin, which is a simple outer clip. If you have a plastic-bonded joint, it needs to be heated to melt the plastic. Use a pick or screwdriver to remove the inner ring clips.

2 Press Out Caps

If you have an arbor press or hydraulic press, pushing the caps out with a socket is easy.

3 Punch Out Caps

If you don't have a press, you can use a vise or the old-fashioned hammer and punch method. A brass punch works great.

4 Remove One Cap

Once the cap on one side is accessible, uses channel locks or other pliers to pull it off.

5 Remove Other Cap

With one cap off, the main body of the joint swivels out of the yoke. The other cap should simply pop out.

6 Place New Cap in Yoke

Press the new cap halfway into the yoke.

7 Install Yoke Joint

Load the body of the joint into the yoke and then insert the other cap into the yoke eye.

8 Press Caps into Yoke

You can press the caps into the yoke if you have a hydraulic or arbor press. Otherwise, you can use a vise or go back to the stone-age with a hammer. Using a socket is the best way to drive the cap into the housing.

9 Install Spring Clips

Use needle-nose pliers to install the new spring clips into the yoke. Make sure they are seated.

10 Install Grease Fitting

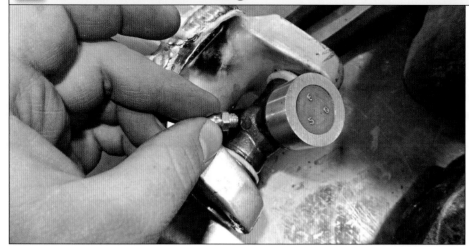

Remember to grease the fitting. Use a 1/4-drive ratchet and whatever socket fits the zerk fitting. Be careful with the zerk fitting, as they are thin and may twist right off. Once the shaft is installed in the car, grease the joint with moly grease.

Snap Rings

Inner and outer snap rings retain the driveshaft to the yoke. The type of yoke determines the type of snap ring. Outer snap rings fit into a groove on the outside of each ear. These are either a full-circle snap ring or the more typical split snap ring that requires special pliers.

Most of the time, U-joint snap rings are full-circle versions and can be removed and installed with needle-nose pliers. Just be sure to set one side of the U-joint against the snap ring before installing the second cap and snap ring. This ensures that there is full engagement and room to install the second ring.

Inner snap rings are trickier and more difficult to install. Each snap ring is a 3/4 ring that must lock into a groove on the inside of the cap where the trunnion seats into the cap. The steel spring is difficult to remove when the U-joint is installed in the shaft. Installation is difficult because the steel resists flexing, but it is certainly not impossible.

When installing inner snap-ring joints, install one cap halfway, load the U-joint body, and then install the second cap. Once the snap ring groove has been exposed on one cap, install the snap ring. Use a vise or press to seat the second cap into place, and press the first snap ring to the inner side of the yoke. Then install the second ring to the second cap.

Project: Modifying a Stock Driveshaft

At some point, you probably will have to deal with a driveshaft that doesn't quite fit. Most builders experience this situation when performing engine/transmission swaps or rear-end swaps. These are most often done in resto-rods. Many restoration projects have had these mods performed already and have to be put back to stock. The driveshaft is a critical component that connects the engine and transmission to the rear differential, so it has to fit just right.

A custom-made driveshaft can cost well over $500; even a stock replacement shaft costs at around $250 to $300. An option is available that does not cost quite so much, and you can do it in your garage: shortening the driveshaft.

First, you figure out the precise length of the driveshaft. With the car on the ground, measure the distance from the center of the rear differential yoke to the tailshaft housing. The weight of the car must be on the rear suspension to get the correct measurement.

Depending on your application, you need a driveshaft that is slightly longer than necessary. If you have swapped in a new transmission, the stock driveshaft may work.

The slip yoke must match the transmission, so you need to check the fitment. You can use conversion U-joints if the U-joint sizes between the slip and rear yokes and the driveshaft yokes are different, but it is best to use a driveshaft with the same yoke size.

The process of shortening it is quite simple. When done correctly, the balance of the shaft should remain. Removing a couple of inches of shaft doesn't change the balance, as long as the driveshaft was balanced at the beginning.

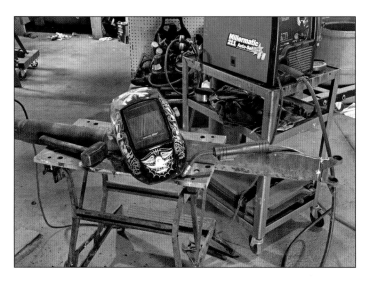

Shortening a driveshaft at home is easy. As long as you don't take off more than a couple of inches or cut the end with the balancing weights, you won't throw off the balance.

1 Place Driveshaft on Workbench

With the shaft supported on a workbench, verify the orientation of the yoke. This is critical to maintaining the balance of the shaft as well as the life of the U-joint. If the yokes are rotated even a few degrees, the shaft will wobble and destroy the U-joints. Make sure the line is long enough to cover the intended shortening area. It doesn't matter which end you shorten, as long as the balance weights are on the opposite end; don't cut them off.

2 Remove Driveshaft Welds

Use a grinder to remove the weld between the shaft and the yoke. It does not take much effort, and you want to keep the grinder closer to the shaft than to the yoke. You can use a cut-off wheel on a die grinder, but an electric grinder is faster.

3 Inspect Yoke and Shaft Separation

This is what you are looking for: the line showing the yoke and shaft separation. You want this line to continue all the way around the yoke.

4 Remove Yoke

A small sledge hammer is all you need to pop out the yoke. Tap around the entire yoke. Don't let the yoke drop to the floor. Catch it with your hand to avoid damaging it.

5 Measure Separation Line

Measure the yoke from the center of the U-joint to the separation line; 2 inches here. This is included in the final length of the shaft.

6 Measure Runout

About 1.5 inches of runout on the slip yoke is the safest amount. This means that, at ride height, 1.5 inches stick out of the transmission. For high-performance cars, this can be as little as 1 inch. Don't get talked into running more than 1.5 inches, though; too much runout causes vibration and can destroy joints and seals. Mark the slip yoke with a line at 1.5 inches. This line will be used for the rest of the measurements.

7 Cut Driveshaft Tube

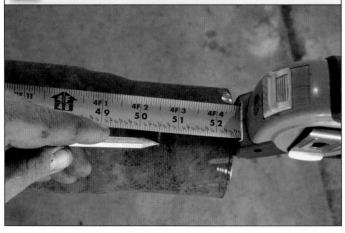

For a shaft that is 52.5 inches long, cut the tube at 50.5 inches. This takes into account that the weld-in yoke is 2 inches from the separation line.

8 Cut Driveshaft Tube (CONTINUED)

Set the shaft in a chop saw and support the long end so that the shaft is level and 90 degrees from the blade. Use a square to check it. There is some room for adjustment, but not much, so you want the cut as square as possible.

9 Grind and Fit Driveshaft Tube

Once cut, the seam on the inside of the tube must be ground down to fit the yoke. A cut-off wheel is perfect for this task.

10 Tap Yoke into Tube

Use a hammer to tap the yoke back into the tube. Make sure the lines match up. This is crucial for a proper balance.

11 Measure Yoke

Measure the yoke at its center as well as at its flat edge to make sure it is not cocked to one side.

12 Measure Yoke Squareness

Check the yoke with a square. Even with accurate measurements, the yoke can be crooked. The square shows if the yoke is true.

13 Tack Weld Driveshaft

Using a MIG welder, place a tack weld at opposite sides of the shaft. The weld needs to be hot enough to penetrate the metal.

14 Weld Driveshaft

Rotate the shaft as you weld it. A single weld is better than several small welds. This shaft is the right length now and should last for the life of the vehicle.

LOCKERS AND SPOOLS

Locker and spool systems are ideally suited for racing and special applications, and in most cases, they can be unnecessary or dangerous for the street. Lockers can handle tons of horsepower into the 1,000-plus range, but most LSDs are maxed out by the time you hit 600 hp. Four-wheel-drive off-road trucks are special-application vehicles and often need constant traction over a variety of terrain. Therefore, many owners use lockers rather than LSD units for off-roading. However, lockers do present some issues on the street because they make a fair amount of noise when turning corners.

Spools, which are not differentials, connect the axles together directly so that they always spin at the same rate. As a result, vehicles with spools struggle to corner effectively and should not be used on the street.

Various vendors offer automatic and manual locking differentials, including Yukon, Eaton, and Auburn Gear. Auto lockers operate similarly to an LSD. When torque is applied to the spider gears, the unit instantly locks the axles together and you get solid lock-up with no slipping. Manual lockers only lock the axles together when told to, via a button on the dash. Manual lockers are either electronic or pneumatic.

A locking differential locks both axles together when torque is applied, ensuring both wheels spin regardless of traction, sending the same power to both wheels, all the time, under power. The automatic lockers open

Here are all the components in a Detroit Locker. A locker operates differently than a limited-slip differential. An LSD functions based on torque and traction; a locker is always coupled under torque, period.

Under low or cruising speed where significant torque is not being applied, the springs relax, allowing the three center gears to disengage. When they unlock and spin against each other, you can hear and feel it. As soon as torque is applied, they instantly lock.

Lockers can be used on the street, but they are noisy. They are best for drag racing and off-roading. If your engine is putting out 700 or more hp, you need a locker for durability. (Photo Courtesy Eaton)

A positive axle-locking differential is well suited for high-performance and special applications and engines that produce 600 to 700 hp. This is the original locker, the Eaton Detroit Locker. (Photo Courtesy Eaton)

the coupling when the driveshaft applies little to no torque to the differential. In cruising or low-speed cornering, no power is applied. As soon as the driver accelerates and torque is applied to the differential, the differential locks. This can cause some handling issues, such as a sideways jerk as the locker engages. Auto lockers are very streetable, but they take some getting used to.

Auto Lockers

An auto locker requires the driver to either adapt his or her driving style or simply live with erratic handling. Manual-transmission cars place different torque loads on the axle assembly than automatics. When a manual transmission applies torque and it is released with every shift, the differential locks and releases. As a result, you get more clunking and banging. As you accelerate out of a corner, the locker freewheels like an open differential until you hit the gas, applying torque; then the locker couples. This places the suspension under different loads and causes erratic handling,

so the car can go into oversteer or understeer condition, which may be difficult for the driver to handle. These characteristics are even more pronounced in wet and snow/ice conditions.

The vehicle application determines whether you need to use a locker. Most street cars simply don't need one. A well-built LSD unit provides the traction needed for street use and works great on the dragstrip or road course as well.

Power handling is big factor for needing a locker. Clutch-type LSDs simply can't handle much more than 450 hp. If you run drag radials or slicks on the track, the tires will provide better traction than street tires and place more of a load on the differential. Then they will fail with even less power. There just isn't enough clutch material and spring pressure to command lock up. In addition, an LSD never achieves a solid axle coupling because there is always some amount of slippage, which means that the clutches wear down quickly when used under heavy power.

A locker does not contain any clutches, so there is nothing to wear out. All lockers operate in a similar fashion. The axles are always coupled together, but a lack of torque allows the axles to spin faster than the main carrier. When a locker operates properly, neither axle can spin slower than the main carrier itself, which is unlike an LSD or open differential. Each axle can, however, spin faster than the carrier, such as the inner wheel in a corner.

Automatic lockers employ different systems to achieve both lock up and release. The most common is the spring type. Eaton pioneered the automatic locker system with its Detroit Locker. With this differential,

the axles are coupled together at all times. However, when there is little to no torque application, the springs on the side of the coupling gears relax and separate enough for them to ratchet tooth to tooth. During a turn, this permits the inner wheel to spin faster than the main carrier, reducing tire chirp. As soon as torque is applied, the springs tighten and the coupling gears snap together.

Mechanical Locking Differentials

Other locking differentials feature flyweight designs, such as the Eaton's mechanical locking differential, the MLocker, also known as a gov-lock. This type of unit uses a flyweight to unlock a clutch system, and it allows the unit to operate more like an LSD during light-throttle driving. When one wheel needs to spin with a speed difference of 100 rpm or more, the flyweight stops, engages the clutches that allow a cam to ramp the side gear, which, in turn, increases pressure on the clutches until the wheels are fully locked. When the differential RPM decreases, the unit returns to unlocked operation. General Motors installed the Eaton G80 gov-lock on many Chevy 4x4 trucks with 10- and 14-bolt rear differentials.

Gov-lock differentials function as they were designed, but durability has been an issue. Although they handle light street duty, they can explode under extreme or racing use. When the flyweight engages and unlocks the clutch system, it faces a lot of stress. If lock-up happens when you get on the throttle hard, the shock can shear the weight, causing the unit to blow apart, which not only destroys most of the internal components of the axle assembly including

Gov-lock differentials were installed in many late-model GM trucks. Although these are adequate for typical street driving, they are not suitable for high-performance or extreme use, such as hard four-wheeling or straight-line acceleration. If used in this manner, the differential responds like a grenade and it will fail spectacularly. You can see the bent pins on the governor mechanism.

When the gov-lock engages under heavy load, the entire carrier differential housing fails and splits apart. Part of the housing is gone and pieces are missing from the gov-lock mechanism. This is a very common failure in GM 8.6 10-bolt differentials.

gears and bearings, but if the axles jamb up against debris, the vehicle can snap sideways and cause a wreck.

You can remove the flyweight and add shims to modify the gov-lock to tighten the cams and clutches. However, it's not a reliable fix for a locking differential, and the gov-lock should not be used in high-performance applications. By the time you get into modifying the G80 differential, you could have a proper LSD or locking differential installed and get the real performance that you need.

Electronic Locking Differentials

These differentials provide the best of both worlds. The open and locked differential is durable and reliable and gives you complete control for its application. They are expensive to purchase and require advanced installation. Selectable and on-command lockers, such as the Eaton ELocker and the ARB Airlocker, use a lever and pneumatic or electric solenoids in the housing to engage the locking mechanism. These dual-type differentials have open-action and locked modes. They eliminate the harshness on the street in open configuration, but at the push of a button, the differential locks and puts full power to the tires regardless of traction. With more function comes more labor on the install side and more cost.

On-command lockers are typically air-, cable-, or electric-solenoid operated, which means you need to run wires and hoses to the differential. The cost is higher for these units, as there are more moving parts and functions to coordinate to make them work. The Eaton ELocker uses 12-volt power to activate an electro-magnetic field that forces the internal collars to move, locking the axles together. Because it is a

On-command lockers, such as this ELocker from Eaton, are either locked or unlocked, depending on the driver. This gives you full control of the differential. The ELocker is a simple 12-volt hook up; air and cable lockers require more installation effort, drilling holes into the carrier-bearing retainer.

This is a four-pinion ELocker, with four gears that climb the two axle spider gears. When the locker is energized, the sliding ring collar engages the axle gears, locking them together. This is the best of both worlds: street comfort and quiet operation, with straight-line positive axle locking, on command. (Photo Courtesy Eaton)

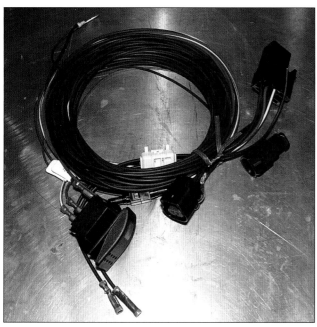

The Eaton ELocker comes with all the wiring necessary to hook it up, including the switch and waterproof connectors. All you need is a 12-volt source that is hot only when the ignition is on.

simple wired application, the installation is much easier than an air- or cable-operated locker.

On-command locker main components are case, flange cap, side gears, pinion or spider gears, clutch gear, spider block, cross shaft, and return springs. The case or the housing holds the ring, pinion, and all other components. The flange cap is the stationary side of the locker, and it operates the locking mechanism. Side gears, similar to an open or LSD unit, connect to the axles and have locking cogs that lock into the clutch gear.

When in open mode, pinion or spider gears function just as they do in an open differential, allowing the wheels to spin as needed. Once the unit is locked, the pinion gears don't move. The clutch gear is the locking gear. When the locker is engaged, the side gears are locked to the case through the clutch gear and this couples both axles together, applying full torque to both wheels. The spider block and cross shafts hold the pinion gears together to operate the unit in open-action mode.

Return springs provide stability for the engage/disengage process for the unit by pushing components together or apart, depending on the configuration of the unit.

The three ways to connect an on-command locker to the driver are lever, air, or electric.

Lever

Lever-actuated units are connected to the axle assembly housing through a cable system. A fork inside the housing cover rides on the locker. When the cable is pulled, the fork actuates the locker and either engages or disengages the unit. These can be fairly complex to install. For off-road vehicles, the cables can snag on trail debris.

Air

Air lockers can be set up in two ways. They use either an air cylinder to operate the engagement fork, or actual air going into the car and directly into the differential. This involves drilling into the case and one of the bearing end caps that holds the carrier to the housing. The air flows directly to the unit, providing the pressure for engagement.

Electric

Eaton ELockers are electronically controlled through a 12-volt switch that operates an internal solenoid inside the carrier. The unit is wired through the case of the axle assembly housing, and the solenoid has a floating ring that slides between the case and the outer carrier bearing. This allows the wire to stay in one place; the circuit is completed through a Torrington bearing. When 12 volts are applied to the solenoid, the locking mechanism is engaged, fully locking the axles together.

Drop-in Lockers

Drop-in lockers are also referred to as "Lunchbox Lockers." They are a budget alternative to a full-on locking carrier. A drop-in unit is an affordable method to couple the axles together while retaining differential action in turns. When one axle needs to spin at a different rate, the unit separates with a ratcheting action much like a full-size locking differential. The difference is that drop-in lockers are very loud; the ratcheting mechanism makes a lot of noise because of the way it works. Some drop-ins have internal dampening springs to help reduce the noise of the ratcheting process.

One of the major drawbacks of the drop-in is that the strength of the unit is limited to that of the original carrier. If the case is not up to the task, it can distort or break. Drop-ins are fairly capable by themselves; the case usually fails before the drop-in unit does.

The drop-in locker is a viable option for tight budgets or for the builder who doesn't want to adjust the critical gear settings. Although not as strong as a full carrier, units such as this Lock-Right from Powertrax (Richmond Gear) work very well. They offer positive locking during straight-line driving, but allow the inside wheel to spin around a corner when needed, such as in street-driven 4x4 trucks and street/strip cars. (Photo Courtesy Powertrax)

Many companies build drop-ins, including Powertrax Lock-Right (made by Richmond Gear), Spartan by Yukon Gear, and Auburn Gear Max Locker. All work on the same basic principle with a few design differences, specifically in the way the spring and locking pin operate. The Lock-Right unit is the only dual-spring drop-in locker, which means it generally has a longer life. The other units are single-spring designs. Some come with new center shafts to hold the unit in the carrier. Spartan lockers do not require side shims, whereas the others do.

Drop-in lockers are good for rock crawlers and moderate off-road vehicles where the expense of a full locker is prohibitive and the power and

weight of the vehicle is less, such as Jeeps and small trucks, although you can buy them for just about any axle assembly. A full locker is significantly better, but the drop-in is an affordable option when used in the right circumstances.

Spools

Spools offer a permanent locking axle, and it's a durable and inexpensive system. Installation is simple and it's lightweight. Nothing is stronger than a spool, but it has poor street manners. The tied axles do not allow the inside rear wheel to spin at a slower rate than the outside wheel.

Spools take the place of the differential and are an excellent, cost-friendly option for a strip-only car. Because the axles are permanently tied together, they spin when the ring gear spins, regardless of anything else. They are cheap, easy to install, and maintenance-free. Another key benefit is weight; a spool weighs only a few pounds while a locker can weight 25 to 30 pounds. That added rotating mass eats up power, so dropping 20 to 25 pounds from the drivetrain could mean the difference between a win and a loss.

The issue comes when trying to make a corner. A spool spins both tires at the same speed, so it makes the inside tire chirp and squeal. That may not be a huge factor if you rarely drive the car on the street, but big tires, a spool, and turns don't mix very well. Most folks who have tried it become tired of it very quickly. Leave the spools on the strip.

Types

Mini and full-weight spools are available. Mini spools are not really suitable for serious drag racing, as

The mini spool is for those who don't want to install a new carrier. It replaces the spider gears, locking the axles together. These spools are not intended for high-horsepower applications (more than 400) or street use. Mini spools are for dirt-track racing only, where there is little to no traction. Do not use them on the street or drag strip because they will break, and that can ruin a whole weekend.

Moser offers several types of spools (left to right): aluminum ultralight, ultra-light steel, full-weight steel, lightened steel. The only difference between a full-weight steel spool and a lightened steel spool is weight; they are equally strong. All of them handle unlimited horsepower, but the aluminum spool eventually wears out the ring-gear bolt holes. (Photo Courtesy Moser Engineering)

they are limited in strength by the stock carrier and crosspin. Mini spools are frequently used on circle track cars. Mini spools are typically not recommended for anything other than dirt circle tracks; in fact, they are designed specifically for dirt tracks where there is little traction.

Full spools are offered in two versions: regular and lightened. Weight is always a consideration when build-ing a drag racing car, so saving every bit of weight possible is beneficial.

A lightened or "ultra-light" spool typically has extra holes drilled in the ring gear mounting pad and inner hub. Some spools have scalloped ring gear pads to further minimize weight. Some ultra-light spools are made from aluminum but these are not suited for high-powered cars; anything beyond 1,000 hp is just too much for an aluminum spool.

Weighing about half of a steel spool, the ring gear support sim-ply cannot withstand much torque. All-aluminum spools must be replaced eventually because they wear out, while a steel spool does not. In fact, most aluminum spools have a limited warranty; most pro steel spools carry a lifetime warranty. Most pro-level spools are made from hard-ened steel, which reduces deflection and increases strength. Pro spools require either a 3.25- or 3.812-inch bore case. Another big advantage of the pro spool is the ability to run larger axles.

WHEELS AND TIRES

Wheel and tire selection and fitment have a big impact on traction and performance so you should choose the wheels that suit your car, application, and rear axle setup. Once the rear differential has been rebuilt, you want to optimize performance and not squander any. Before making your purchase, you should have an entire build-up plan; tires and wheels should be part of that plan.

Wheel sizing has a dramatic effect on the overall plan. Chassis mods, brake sizing, and suspension settings will alter the available room in the wheel wells. First things first, you need to measure the stock wheels.

Wheel Fitment

The tendency is to get the biggest tires that will possibly fit into the wheel wells. You need to be sure that the offset and backspacing are correct for the width of the axle and the size of the wheel well. Once you buy wheels and have tires mounted, you cannot return them if you made a mistake. To measure a wheel, you need a long straightedge and a measuring tape. Place the straightedge along the back lip of the wheel, preferably without a tire. If you can't take the tire off, air it down and press the straightedge to the steel. Using the measuring tape, place the leading edge to the wheel-mounting flange. To measure backspacing, measure where the wheel contacts the rotor or hub. If the tire is off the wheel, measure the overall width of the inside of the wheel hoop, bead to bead (where the tire seats). To measure front spacing, measure the front side of the wheel as you did the rear side. Wheels are typically made only in .5-inch increments (6, 6.5, 7, etc.). Add these two together and you have the wheel's width. The wheel diameter will be fairly obvious if you have a tire, if not, measure the outer diameter of the wheel hoop at its widest point.

Wheel Offset

The wheel offset is another key

Many stock GM muscle cars, such as the Chevelle, were equipped with Chevy 12-bolt differentials but the stock wheel size was either 14 or 15 inches. Many owners with upgraded differentials select 17- or 18-inch wheels for higher performance because the larger wheels provide a bigger footprint and more traction. (Photo Courtesy Paul Johnson)

Wheels and tires that fit the vehicle correctly provide the necessary traction for the application. This 1981 Chevy truck has 20-inch wheels and off-road tires that are a touch too big. The fender sits directly over the tread blocks, so, as soon as the suspension compresses, the tires scrub. Offset is an important factor in determining the correct wheels; if it's wrong, it can ruin your project.

Wheels are the final drive component of the rear axle and you must match the wheel size, offset, and backspacing so you attain the correct performance characteristics. In addition, the wheels need to fit under the bodywork of the car.

Several key measurements determine the best wheels for your vehicle. Most aftermarket wheels have a tag on the inside of the wheel. This is a 15-inch-diameter wheel, 8 inches wide with 4.75 inches of backspacing and a 5-lug 4.5-inch bolt pattern. Most GM cars and trucks that have 10- or 12-bolt differentials use 5-on-4.75, 5-on-5, or 5-on-6 lug bolt patterns.

element. The wheel offset is the distance from the hub-mounting surface to the centerline of the wheel. Matching the stock backspacing and offset will yield no effect on the car's handling or scrub radius. The scrub radius is the point at which the tire and wheel clear everything in the suspension. As the wheel widens, the scrub radius decreases and the wheel comes closer to the suspension components. Therefore, you have to measure the offset to ensure that the wheels fit and clear all of the components and the inner wheel well. The stock wheels and offset are designed so that the wheel centerline intersects with the suspension component angle at ride height. This provides the best handling.

The three types of offset are zero, positive, and negative. To measure offset, you need to know the backspacing, wheel's width, and wheel centerline. To determine the centerline, simply divide the wheel width by two. In order to determine the wheel offset, you simply subtract the wheel centerline measurement from the backspacing measurement. If

If the wheel doesn't have a sticker, the measurements should be stamped on the inside of the wheel. The backspacing number is not usually provided as part of the stamping.

To find the backspacing, lay a straightedge across the outer lip of the wheel and measure down to the wheel-mounting pad.

the backspacing is less than the centerline, the offset is negative. If the backspacing is greater than the centerline, the offset is positive.

Changing the offset has mixed results. Running a smaller offset pushes the wheel outward, which widens the track width. The wider the track width, the more stable the car becomes, to a point. Eventually, the tire gets too close to the fender and scrubs the fender in turns and may also rub during suspension articulation. A smaller offset allows for an overall wider wheel, which increases drag, but the benefits of a more stable front end outweigh the drag increase. For show-oriented cars, filling the wheel wells is important, and a small offset does that because it pushes the tire and wheel outward.

Pulling the wheel inward, running a larger offset runs into other issues, such as suspension clearance. Rubbing the tire against the suspension components is really not a good idea. You have to be careful when selecting the wheel size. When increasing the wheel width, it is a good idea to add half of the width to the backspacing to maintain the original offset and prevent any suspension contact. Going from a 15 x 7 with 4.5-inch backspacing to a 15 x 8 with 5-inch backspacing maintains the offset, as long as that extra inch still clears everything.

Measuring the bolt circle is probably the most confusing, but it is fairly easy. When measuring five-lug wheels, you run the tape across the 1 and 3 holes. A hole will be directly above the tape. Always measure from the outer edge of one bolt hole to the center of the opposing bolt hole. For even-numbered patterns, you measure center to center, directly across from each other. The same goes for the wheel studs on the rotor or drum.

The wheel diameter is typically the measurement between the tire beads and not between the outer wheel lips.

The wheel width is the measurement between the wheel lips, not between the outer lips.

Bolt patterns are difficult to measure because even- and odd-number lug patterns are measured differently. For even patterns, such as this six-lug GM pattern, you measure from the center of one stud to the center of the one directly across from it. This is a 6-on-5.5-inch pattern. We burned an inch to get an accurate measurement.

Odd-number patterns, such as this five-lug, are measured from the edge of one stud to the center of the stud across from it (not to the stud next to it). This is a 5-on-4.5-inch pattern.

Wheel Size

To determining ideal wheel size takes some more measuring. Although it was stated that picking out the wheels should be the first thing you do, it does not necessarily mean that you need to buy them yet. If you plan on making significant changes to the suspension, front or rear, those changes need to be made before you buy the wheels. Front suspension components that can get in the way are tie-rod ends, A-arms, brake calipers, shocks and mounts, as well as the inner and outer fenders.

Caliper overhang is the first dimension to check. This is the clearance between the outer side of the caliper and the inner side of the wheel face. Wheel drop is where the hoop steps in to meet the center section; this affects caliper clearance as well. You also need to determine the caliper radial clearance, and that's the height of the caliper in relation to the center-line of the hub. As a general rule, you should have a minimum of 1/4-inch of clearance between any brake or suspension component. Aftermarket brake manufacturers list the smallest wheel diameter that fits their particular rotors and calipers, but you cannot rely solely on these specs so you need to measure the wheels to ensure fitment. You can simply bolt up wheels that should fit to verify fitment, but remember that you cannot return tires that have been mounted.

Project: Creating a Wheel Fitment Jig

Although you can buy special tools to check tire and wheel fitment, you can easily build a jig yourself using simple parts you probably already have on hand.

Use a long piece of angle aluminum (or steel), long enough to extend to the full radius of the tire/wheel combo you are considering. If you are using a 17-inch wheel with a 27-inch tire, your angle aluminum needs to reach at least 30 inches. You must consider the bolt circle diameter into the length, as the angle will bolt across two bolts. Drill one end to fit across two lugs (not as you would measure the bolt pattern, but to clear the hub), and slot the opposite end.

Using a piece of all-thread, a couple of washers and nuts, thread the all-thread through the angle. Because the end is slotted, you can adjust the rod to the wheel diameter and the tire diameter. Using this tool, you can rotate the rotor and find out where the rod hits something. Continue pulling the all-thread out until it clears everything, inside and outside.

Measure the length inward and outward, and you will have the tire and wheel fitment specs. The front suspension is a little tricky, as it moves throughout its travel in an arc, so you have to make some concessions. All measurements must be made with the suspension at ride height.

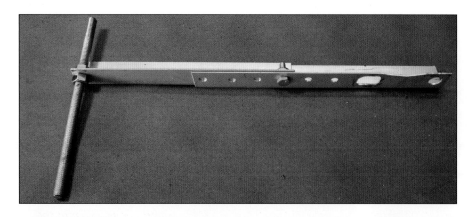

To measure the car, you can build this wheel fitment tool from some aluminum angle, a piece of all-thread, and some nuts and bolts. The wheel width measurements are designated in several increments.

1 Choose Tool Type

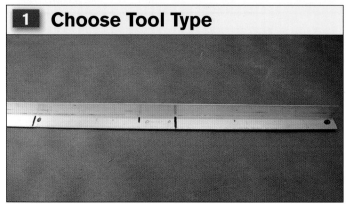

You need to figure out the type of measurement tool you want to make. You can make one for a specific application or several applications. The piece of angle aluminum must fit over two wheel studs. I marked several points for cutting. You can make this adjustable to fit a lot of different applications. This one is spec'd for a 33-inch tire maximum. The large line in the center is where the angle will be cut into two pieces.

2 Cut Aluminum to Desired Length

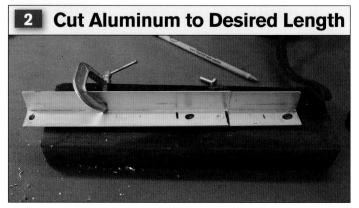

The tool telescopes to measure several vehicles. Use a bolt and nut to clamp the two pieces of aluminum together in the desired position. I determined that the minimum diameter of this tool is 18 inches, but you can make it as big or small as you want. Clamp the halves together to set the shortest diameter. Leave enough room for the lug pattern. Drill the piece of aluminum at the correct distance to fit the lug pattern. I made this particular tool to fit all five- and six-lug patterns.

3 Drill Lug Holes

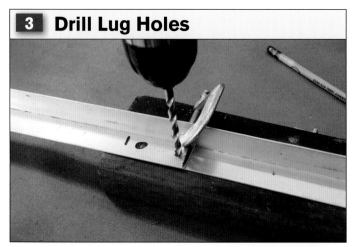

Drill the two pieces at the same time to ensure that they match. The piece to the left is the extension, the piece on the right is the base. I used a 1/4-inch bolt to hold them together.

4 Mark Base for Lugs

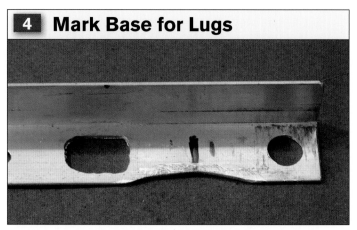

This base is marked for two lugs and the center of the wheel line. The upper lug hole is slotted so that it will fit more than one wheel. This tool fits 5-on-4.5, -4.75, and -5 patterns, as well the small GM six-lug pattern.

5 Mark Wheel for Reference

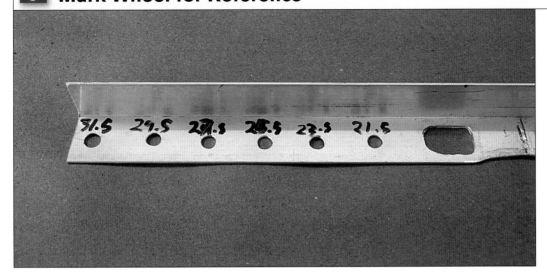

Mark the center of the wheel and the lower half for the various diameters. This particular tool is for measuring tire clearance. Use the tire diameter, divide by two to get the radius and then subtract the length of the extension piece. Measure from the center of the wheel to each diameter, and drill. This tool is marked from 21.5 to 31.5 in 2-inch increments.

6 Insert Bolt Extension

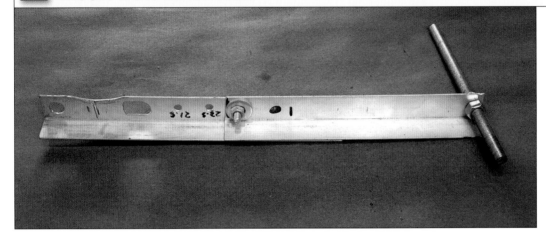

Use a piece of 5/16-inch all-thread on the extension section. This can be whatever width you need. Connect the two halves with a 1/4-20 bolt. This tool measures the diameter and tire/wheel clearance from the wheel-mounting surface. You can get any measurement necessary with this tool.

Project: Measuring for Tire Clearance

1 Set Up Tool

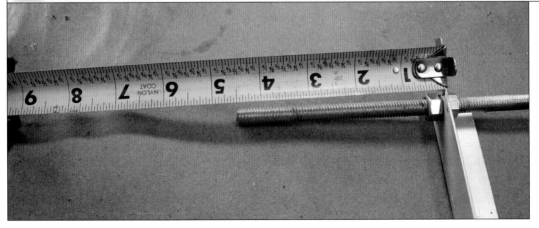

This example, a 10-inch tire on a 10-inch-wide wheel with a 4.5-inch backspace, shows 4.5 inches of inner tire. You need to factor in the backspacing and overall tire width. The all-thread can measure backspacing and tire-to-fender well/wheel lip clearance by simply threading out the right amount of rod.

2 Attach Tool to Hub

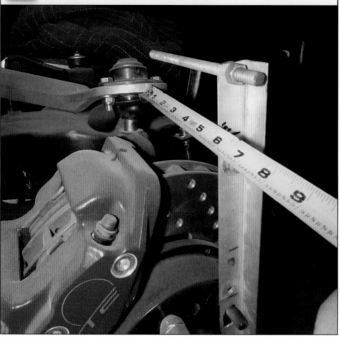

Mount the measurement tool to the wheel hub. A 1966 Corvette is shown. With the tool set to its lowest point, there are just 5 inches of space between the upper A-arm and an 18-inch wheel.

3 Check Front Clearance

Turn the wheels in and out, lock to lock, and check a full rotation for clearance. You want to find the maximum width and diameter. The rule is to add 1 inch overall width and diameter for tire growth at highway speed. That means you want a minimum of 1/2-inch clearance on both sides.

4 Check Rear Clearance

The same process works out back. This Corvette has just 5 inches of clearance to the sway bar, severely limiting the width of the rear wheel.

5 Verify Clearance

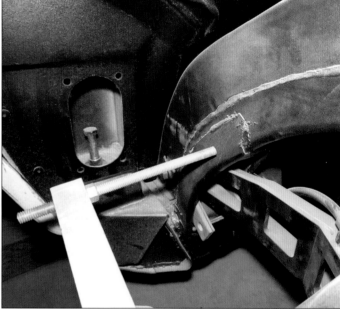

At 28 inches of diameter, the tire has just 5 inches of clearance to the frame, but at 27 inches, there is more than 6 inches of clearance. It pays to check, as a 27-inch tire can be 1 inch wider than a 28-inch-tall tire.

Wheel Construction

Choosing the right wheels depends on your style. However, wheel construction is just as important as the design. Steel wheels, regardless of whether they are aftermarket or factory, are fairly heavy. The rotational forces compound the weight of the wheels and a large-diameter tire adds a lot of inertia to the rest of the car. This is important because upgrading the wheels and tires from stock changes the dynamics a little. Aluminum is lighter than steel, cast aluminum is about a third lighter, and forged aluminum is even lighter still.

Wheel Diameter

The diameter of the wheel also plays a role in braking performance. Because aluminum wheels are lighter, you can typically run a larger wheel with a similar-size low-profile tire as on a steel wheel but without having any braking issues. The rotating force is similar because the tire diameter remains the same and the alloy wheel weighs less. Once you go beyond those specs, your wheels put an extra burden on the braking system. A 22-inch wheel with a 40-series tire is much more difficult to stop than a 15-inch wheel and a 60-series tire.

Tire Codes

Tire sizing codes have long been a sticking point; they seem confusing. In reality, the codes are simple and easy to follow if you know the system.

As an example here is the code breakdown for a 245/40R17 967 tire:

245	cross-section width in millimeters
40	aspect ratio in percent
R	radial construction
17	Rim diameter; 17 inches
96	Load index; 96 represents 1,565 pounds
Z	Speed rating; Z represents 149+ mph

The load index number is the overall load capacity of the tire; the minimum is 71. The speed rating is important for street machines. This spec notes the maximum sustainable speed for a 10-minute period.

You can easily find your tire height with this formula:

$$H = W \times A \div 25.4 \times 2 + D$$

Where:
H = height of sidewall
W = width of tire
A = aspect ratio
25.4 = factor to convert to inches
2 = number of sidewalls
D = diameter of rim

Aluminum Wheel Build Types

In addition to the steel wheel (which is typically two-piece welded construction), there are four main build types for aluminum wheels: cast, forged, billet, and multi-piece. Each has its own pros and cons.

Cast

Molten aluminum is poured into forms to make cast wheels; these wheels are the most affordable and heaviest of all the aluminum wheels. This is a quick way to make a wheel, but at the same time this makes for a more fragile wheel. Curb-checks and potholes are mortal enemies of the cast wheel. If one breaks, it can't be repaired. Cast wheels are also typically painted or chromed, which eventually chips and flakes, resulting a bad look.

Forged

Here, a slug of aluminum is forced into a form under extreme pressure to take the shape of the new wheel. This process uses several dies and takes time to manufacture. The wheels are then machined to the final fit and finish. Of all the aluminum wheels, forged wheels are the lightest, the strongest, and the most expensive. That said, the designs are more limited because of the manufacturing processes. When bent or damaged, these wheels can generally be repaired.

Billet

These wheels are made of high-quality solid aluminum stock and then machined to the final fit and finish. This produces a lot of waste aluminum and it takes a long time to produce a single wheel. This makes them more expensive than cast wheels, but they are quite strong. Billet wheels are nearly as strong as forged wheels but weigh a little more. The increased rolling mass can be an issue with large-diameters (20-inch or greater) and stock brakes.

Multi-piece

These can be a combination of any of the above constructions. Most often, the hoop is forged or billet and the center is one of the other forms. A cast center piece is not as strong, but that portion of the wheel is less likely to fail than the hoop. A cast hoop with a cast center is not as good. ∎

You can uses these codes to determine the DOT ratings. The codes are molded into the side of every DOT-approved tire made.

Also molded on the sidewall is the size, speed rating, and the weight load rating.

If you plug in the numbers from the example above, 245/40R17 96Z, the overall height of this tire is 24.72 inches (245 x .40 ÷ 25.4 x 2 + 17). But remember that each tire has variations due to the manufacturer tolerances and design.

Tire Grading

The Uniform Tire Quality Grading ratings (UTQG) list three components, treadwear, traction, and temperature.

Treadwear

The treadwear grade specifies tire wear according to controlled testing conditions on a government test track. A tire graded at 400 lasts twice as long as a tire graded at 200. High-performance tires are typically in the low 300s to high 200s, whereas ultra-high-performance tires run in the low 200s. This means that the tires do not last as long as a 400-rated tire under normal conditions. Doing smoky burnouts on 400-rated tires every time you leave a stoplight is going to seriously reduce the life of the tire.

Traction

The traction grades are rated from C (the lowest) to B, A, and AA (the highest). The ratings refer to the tire's ability to stop on wet pavement under controlled test conditions.

Temperature

The temperature grades are A (the highest), B, and C. This spec indicates the tire's resistance to the generation of heat.

Tire Use

Choosing the right tire for your application is determined by how you intend to use the car. A drag car needs sticky rear tires for traction with narrow front tires to reduce drag; a road course car needs sticky, wide tires at each corner for better handling; and a street machine needs a little of both. How you drive, where you live, and when you use your street machine all have an effect on what tires you need. DOT-legal street slicks are great for the occasional cruise night on warm summer evenings, but toss in some rain and things can become intense quickly.

Evaluate how you will use your street machine before buying your tires.

Most builders look at two main categories, high performance and ultra-high performance. A high-performance-level tire has slightly less grip, but the tread wears better, and most are all-season tires, so they handle well in the wet and the dry.

Ultra-high-performance tires have lower UTQG treadwear ratings, so they wear out faster, but they handle much better. Less sidewall deflection, better grip, and aggressive tread is perfect for a high-powered street machine with the ability to corner well. Ultra-high performance tires, almost as a rule, are not designed for snow. Not that many street machines get driven in the snow, but if you live where it is at all possible to get caught in a snowstorm in your street machine, you might as well be driving with slicks at each corner because they are that bad.

Low-profile tires on aluminum wheels can be damaged easily on rough rural roads or roads with pot holes. Aluminum wheels bend pretty easily and cast wheels can even break. One of the benefits of a taller sidewall

Tire Sizes

The following tire suggestions come from Vintage Wheel Works and are based on factory ride height, suspension brakes, and sheet metal. These tire sizes are known to fit the vehicles listed, with no clearance issues.

1967–1968 Camaro

Wheel Size	Tire Size
15 x 4	No specific tire recommendations
15 x 7	195 or 205 or 225/60/15 front and rear
16 x 7	195 or 205 or 225/50/16 front and rear
16 x 8	205 or 225/50/16 front and rear
16 x 8	245/50/16 rear only
17 x 7	195 or 205 or 225/40/17 front and rear
17 x 8	205 or 225/40/17 front and rear
17 x 8	245/40/17 rear only

1969 Camaro

Wheel Size	Tire Size
15 x 4	No specific tire recommendations
15 x 7	195 or 205 or 225/60/15 front and rear
15 x 8	245 or 255/60/15 rear only
16 x 7	195 or 205 or 225/50/16 front and rear
16 x 8	205 or 225 or 245 or 255/50/16 front and rear
17 x 7	195 or 205 or 225/40/17 front and rear
17 x 8	205 or 225 or 245 or 255/40/17 front and rear

1970–1982 Camaro

Wheel Size	Tire Size
15 x 4	No specific tire recommendations
15 x 7	195 or 205 or 225/60/15 front and rear
16 x 7	195 or 205 or 225/50/16 front and rear
16 x 8	205 or 225/50/16 front and rear
16 x 8	245/50/16 rear only
17 x 7	195 or 205 or 225/40/17 front and rear
17 x 8	205 or 225/40/17 front and rear
17 x 8	245/40/17 rear only

1963–1967 Corvettes

Wheel Size	Tire Size
15 x 4	No specific tire recommendations
15 x 7	195 or 205 or 225/60/15 front and rear
16 x 7	195 or 205 or 225/50/16 front and rear
16 x 8	205 or 225/50/16 front and rear
17 x 7	195 or 205 or 225/40/17 front and rear
17 x 8	205 or 225/40/17 front and rear

1968–1982 Corvettes

Wheel Size	Tire Size
15 x 4	No specific tire recommendations
15 x 7	195 or 205 or 225/60/15 front and rear
15 x 8	245/60/15 rear only
16 x 7	195 or 205 or 225/50/16 front and rear
16 x 8	225 or 245/50/16 front and rear
16 x 8	255/50/16 rear only
17 x 7	195 or 205 or 225/40/17 front and rear
17 x 8	205 or 225 or 245/40/17 front and rear
17 x 8	255/40/17 rear only

1964–1966 GTO

Wheel Size	Tire Size
15 x 4	No specific tire recommendations
15 x 7	195 or 205 or 225/60/15 front and rear
15 x 8	245/60/15 rear only
16 x 7	195 or 205 or 225/50/16 front and rear
16 x 8	205 or 225 or 245/50/16 front and rear
17 x 7	195 or 205 or 225/40/17 front and rear
17 x 8	205 or 225 or 245/40/17 front and rear ■

Tire Load Capacity

Load Index	Pounds	Kilograms	Load Index	Pounds	Kilograms	Load Index	Pounds	Kilograms
71	761	345	84	1,102	500	98	1,653	750
72	783	355	85	1,135	515	99	1,709	775
73	805	365	86	1,168	530	100	1,764	800
74	827	375	87	1,201	545	101	1,819	825
75	853	387	88	1,235	560	102	1,874	850
76	882	400	89	1,279	580	103	1,929	875
77	908	412	90	1,323	600	104	1,984	900
78	937	425	91	1,356	615	105	2,039	925
79	963	437	92	1,389	630	106	2,094	950
80	992	450	93	1,433	650	107	2,149	975
81	1,019	462	94	1,477	670	108	2,205	1,000
82	1,047	475	95	1,521	690	109	2,271	1,030
83	1,074	487	96	1,565	710	110	2,337	1,060
			97	1,609	730			

is more give for potholes and road debris. Of course, increased sidewall deflection is one of the biggest drawbacks; a 50-series tire (50 percent shorter than the overall width) is a good place to start. The 35-series tires look great, but the ride is a little harsh.

Tire Construction

Studying each tire by its construction is a critical step in deciding what you need. Tires are not created equally; in fact, they are all different, depending on the intended use. Bolt-ing a set of wrinkle-wall slicks on a road car would mean disaster by the first turn. You have to know what you are going to do with them before you click the "buy it now" button.

Street Tires

For street cars, you are looking at DOT-rated tires. These are tires that have passed the strict DOT regulations for street use. Wrinkle-wall tires *do not* meet this description. Just because a tire is DOT rated does not mean that it is a good idea to drive it on the street.

To be approved for street use, a tire must meet standards, specifically hydroplane resistance, tread depth, and sidewall stiffness. The bare minimum tread depth is 2/32 inch for street use; most drag radials are in the standard operating range of 5/32 with 10/32 for a street tire.

Tire compound is also a factor, but most DOT track tires use a special compound that is sticky enough for the track and safe enough for driving home.

Speed Rating

Code	MPH	KM/H	Code	MPH	KM/H
A1	3	5	L	75	120
A2	6	10	M	81	130
A3	9	15	N	87	140
A4	12	20	P	94	150
A5	16	25	Q	100	160
A6	19	30	R	106	170
A7	22	35	S	112	180
A8	25	40	T	118	190
B	31	50	U	124	200
C	37	60	H	130	210
D	40	65	V	149	240
E	43	70	Z	over 149	over 240
F	50	80	W	168	270
G	56	90	(W)	over 168	over 270
J	62	100	Y	186	300
K	68	110	(Y)	over 186	over 300

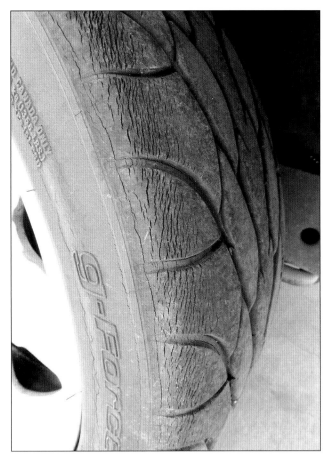

You need to pay attention to the condition of your tires. This shows a potentially dangerous situation that many people don't think of. These tires only have a few thousand miles on them, but they are five to six years old, and the weather cracks in them will significantly reduce their usable life. Driving hard makes this worse, especially on low-profile tires such as this one.

whether you have a clutch or torque convertor. Carl Robinson of Mickey Thompson Tires told me, "A clutch car works much better with bias-ply ET Street tires. I'm not saying radials don't work, but it takes a sophisticated clutch and suspension to take advantage of the reduced rolling resistance of a radial early in the run." He also said that power adders with stock suspension cars have really encouraged the use of tubes in bias-ply tires. The tubes provide additional support for the bias construction, improving the grip of the contact patch.

Radials Versus Bias-Plys

Most manufacturers have a disclaimer about not mixing bias-ply tires and radials on the same car. This is true for street driving, but drag racing is different. You don't have to deal with corners and bumps in drag racing, which is where the two designs are drastically different. You need a set of street radials to drive you car to and from the track when you are racing with bias-ply DOT drag tires.

Rubber Compounds

Every manufacturer has proprietary rubber compounds. The tread compound not only determines the life of the tire, but also the length of the burnout. Regular street tires typically do not easily withstand burnouts; the heat makes them greasy and slick, although some high-performance street tires (such as the BFGoodrich Radial TA KDW) like a short little burnout. Drag tires, however, usually require some level of burnout to heat them up.

Again, every brand is different. Mickey Thompson suggests the tires be heated to within 15 degrees of the track temperature. Drag radials

Drag Tires

There are two kinds of DOT drag tires: radials and bias-plys. Drag radials provide a sturdy sidewall for cornering and ride. They also have less rolling resistance than bias-ply tires. The caveat to a drag radial is the compound. They use a special soft compound, which is good for the track, but driving them on the street is going to eat them pretty quickly, especially if you enjoy the occasional "spirited" stoplight to stoplight run.

It is important to note that some manufacturers expressly label their DOT drag tires as drag race use only. Not all DOT drag tires are capable of safely getting you home; they are built for drag racing only, and just barely meet the DOT specs.

Some manufacturers market their DOT drag tires specifically for

the "drive to the track and race on the same tires" crowd, which is how it should be. BFGoodrich and Mickey Thompson drag radials have the most tread in this group. The G-Force radial was designed for straight-line performance along with high-speed stability and cornering performance for streetability.

The point is that you have to decide what you need. If you trailer the car and need a DOT tire for class restrictions, choosing a non-streetable tire is acceptable, but if you want to drive the car home after a day of racing, you need a tire that has some realistic street capabilities.

Transmission Type

The transmission type is an important factor to consider when selecting your tire design, or rather,

Bias-Ply Roll-Out

Bias-ply tires are made with nylon cords that crisscross. Over time, the cords shrink, reducing the rolling height of the tire. Bias-ply tires must be matched within 1/2 inch of each other.

Tire pressure in a drag tire is crucial for launch and traction control. Although 35 psi is optimum for street driving, running that much pressure on the track will leave you spinning off the line. Every car is different and every tire is different, so experimentation is required, but there are some starting guidelines.

Mickey Thompson suggests keeping a logbook of air pressures and suspension settings with each run (you should be doing this anyway) to determine what your best pressure is. The website lists each tire with its minimum suggested tire pressure by vehicle weight.

For example, a 28-inch-tall Pro Drag Radial on a 3,200-pound car should run a minimum of 12 psi; the same tire on a 2,800-pound car can go as low as 10 psi.

They are even more specific for the ET Street radials with a specific range of air pressure for 275 and smaller (14 to 18 psi) and 296 and larger tires (12 to 16 psi). These numbers can be used as a good starting point for other brands as well, but Mickey Thompson claims that their tires tend to perform better with a little more pressure than other brands. ∎

need less burnout because the special compounds that make them streetable becomes gummy when they are heated too much. In fact, the ET Street and Street Radial tires only need a short spin to haze the tires because they heat up quickly. This brings the special compounds to the surface, increasing the stickiness of the tire.

Although you may miss out on the big nasty smoke show, you are saving the life of your tires and you will go faster, which is what it is all about. Let the guy who doesn't know any better burn off his tires to get loose.

BFGoodrich recommends a light spin to clean up the rubber and put a little haze on as well. If you put too much heat on them they start to ball up, kind of like little balls of goo you get when you rub an adhesive. These can actually work against you, slowing the car in the first 60 feet. In the end, you need to take the manufacturer's suggestions and experiment with your car.

Longevity

Another aspect of the rubber compound is tire longevity. For a fully sponsored racer, tires are not an issue, but for the average Joe, a set of tires needs to last as long as possible. When I asked about the life expectancy of drag radials, Carl's reply was, "Would that be the first or the third set?"

On average, the life of a set of drag radials with a mix of track time and highway miles is between 3,000 and 5,000 miles. To provide the grip, the compound is considerably softer than a stock style or even an ultra-high performance street tire. That grip comes at a cost of lifespan. It all depends on how often you are going to run the drag tires. Also, keeping them properly stored for the majority of the time will certainly add to the life of the tire.

Every tire has a tire wear rating as part of the UTQG required by the DOT. This rating is based on the tests performed by the National Highway Traffic Safety Administration (NHTSA) over a specific 400-mile loop, driven for 7,200 miles in west Texas. The numbers range from zero to more than 600. A typical street tire has a treadwear rating in the 400 to 600 range. These tires last a long time, providing a comfortable ride in all weather conditions.

The general rule is that every time you double up on the tread-wear rating, the tire will last twice as long: a 400 lasts twice as long as a 200. A BFGoodrich Radial TA (the classic muscle car tire) has a treadwear rating of 400. The ultra-high-performance street version of the TS, the G-Force TA KDW, is rated at 300, and the ultra-sticky G-Force TA Drag Radial features a 00 treadwear rating. Although these standards leave some room for interpretation, a 00 rating means that the tire did not last the entire course; it performed under street conditions, not racing.

Here's a puzzle: The G-Force KDW has an AA traction rating, which means that on asphalt the tire pulls more than .54 G, and more than .41 G on concrete.

On the other hand, the Drag Radial, with its sticky compound, has a B rating. This is because drag radials are not designed for wet traction, and the DOT traction test is based on wet traction.

Temperature Resistance

This grading number is actually an important detail for a drag tire.

The temperature of a tire increases as speed and time at that speed increases. The ratings are A, B, and C. (Do not confuse these ratings with the speed ratings, which measure only speed.) All tires in the United States must be rated at a C or better, which means that the tire is capable of 85 to 100 mph without damage. The B rating is 100 to 115 mph, and A is faster than 115 mph.

Of course, even though a drag radial is capable of handling well over 100 mph, it is not capable of these speeds for long durations. It is not advisable to drive a car on drag radials at elevated speeds for prolonged periods as the temperature buildup could cause them to fail in a spectacular fashion.

Tire Sizing

You would have to be living in a hole in the middle of nowhere to not know about the existence of 17-inch and larger wheels. The days of the 15-inch wheel are almost completely gone, save for the sportsman drag racer. Because of the proliferation of 17- to 20-inch wheels in motorsports, there is a need for drag tires that fit those wheels. Mickey Thompson, Nitto, BFGoodrich, and Hoosier offer large-diameter DOT drag radials. In fact, Nitto's NT05R is only available in 17- to 20-inch sizes.

The main reason for stepping into a larger wheel is because of the large rear-wheel disc brakes that require it, particularly on the late-model cars, such as Vipers, Corvettes, etc. There is, however, a trade-off with larger wheels, and that is something you need to consider for your street machine.

A steep-geared dragster can handle 30-inch tires, but throw those on a car with 3.73 gears, and you will know what slow is. The Nitto NT05R 20-inch tire is a 315/35R20, with a 28.74-inch overall diameter and 12.48 width; this is far from the 10.5 tire that many street car classes require.

That 28.74 inch-diameter means you have about 4 inches of sidewall ($28.74 - 20 \div 2 = 4.37$). The same-diameter tire in a 15-inch wheel yields 6.5 inches of sidewall. That extra 2 inches of sidewall is a lot of room for extra traction.

Radial-tire sidewalls may be stiff, but they still flex a little, providing the wider contact patch that you want. When at all possible, run the smallest wheel that your brakes allow. This maximizes the sidewall height, putting more power to the ground. It may not "look" as cool, but your quicker timeslip will look much better.

Tire Storage

The final thing to consider in relation to tires is how to store them. Some of it depends on the design of the tire. Bias-ply tires are not stable enough to sit inflated with the car on them for long periods; flat spots develop quickly. Radial tires do not have this problem, but you still need to take care of them in the off-season. All drag radials are considered summer dry-weather tires, so there is no reason to keep them on your car when it is wet and cold outside.

Bias-ply tires should be stored either off the car or with the car suspended so the load is off the tires. Drop the tire pressure to 5 psi. To pro-

tect the tires from UV damage, keep them covered and out of direct sunlight. Fluorescent light can damage them as well. Another tip is to keep them away from electric motors. Electric motors generate ozone, which eats rubber. There is also no need to use tire dressings; just clean the sidewalls with mild detergent and rinse; leave the tread surface alone.

Radials are not as sensitive as bias-ply tires, but many of the same principles apply. You can leave radials under pressure, but if you take them off the car and air them down, they last longer. The best environment for the rubber is the same as for a bias-ply: no light, no electric motors in close proximity. Clean them with soap and rinse them well.

Tire Selection

There are significant differences among DOT tires, so you need to find the one that suits your vehicle, setup, and application. The key to making the right selection for your car is to know what your car needs to go fast. Remember that street tires allow the tires to slip; drag tires don't.

If you have a weak link, slicks and drag radials will find it and point it out to you in spectacular fashion. A weak axle setup will break under the load of sticky tires. You could end up going more slowly because your car needs to spin the tires a little to go faster.

When upgrading to a drag tire, other rules apply that you must adhere to in order to pass tech, such as axle and lug nut specs. As long as you adhere to the rules and practice safe racing, you will go faster.

SOURCE GUIDE

BF Goodrich
P.O. Box 19001
Greenville, SC 29602
877-788-8899
bfgoodrichtires.com

Currie Enterprises
382 N. Smith
Corona, CA 92880
714-528-6957
currieenterprises.com

Danaher Tool Group
14600 York Rd., Ste. A
Sparks, MD 21152
800-688-8949
gearwrench.com

Eaton Corporation
1111 Superior Ave.
Cleveland, OH 44114
216-523-5000
eaton.com

Loctite Consumer Products
26235 First St.
Westlake, OH 44145
800-624-7767
loctiteproducts.com

Mcgard
3875 California Rd.
Orchard Park, NY 14127
716-662-8980
mcgard.com

Mickey Thompson Performance
4600 Prosper Dr.
Stow, OH 44224
330-928-9092
mickeythompsontires.com

Moser Engineering
102 Performance Dr.
Portland, IN 47371
260-726-6689
moserengineering.com

Randy's Ring & Pinion
10411 Airport Rd.
Everett, WA 98204
1-800-292-1031
ringpinion.com

Ratech
11110 Adwood Dr.
Cincinnati, OH 45240
513-742-2111
ratechmfg.com

Royal Purple, Inc.
One Royal Purple Ln.
Porter, TX 77365
888-382-6300
royalpurple.com

Stainless Steel Brakes Company
11470 Main Rd.
Clarence, NY 14031
800-448-7722
ssbrakes.com

Strange Engineering
8300 N. Austin Ave.
Morton Grove, IL 60053
847-663-1701
strangeengineering.net

Summit Racing
P.O. Box 909
Akron, OH 44398
800-230-3030
summitracing.com

Yukon Gear & Axle
10411 Airport Rd.
Everett, WA 98204
888-905-5044
yukongear.com